THE
>>>>> BREAKFORTH <<<<<
PRINCIPLE

THE >>>>> **BREAKFORTH** <<<<< PRINCIPLE

Build The Inner Leader Your Organization Needs Now!

Nichelle L. Early

BreakForth Press

A Division of BreakForth Publishing Group
Haymarket, VA

First Edition

Published by BreakForth Press
A Division of BreakForth Publishing Group
www.BreakForthPublishingGroup.com

Hardcover ISBN: 979-8-9952134-0-6
Paperback ISBN: 979-8-9952134-1-3
EBook ISBN: 979-8-9952134-2-0

Library of Congress Control Number: 2026908263

Author: Nichelle L. Early

Cover Design: Wesley R. Bryant
Interior Design: Jessica Benjamin-Purmeswar
Editor: Dr. Terri Gibson

This publication is intended for informational, inspirational, and educational purposes only. It is not intended to provide legal, financial, medical, psychological, therapeutic, or other professional advice. Readers should consult qualified professionals regarding their individual circumstances. The views expressed in this book are those of the author alone and do not necessarily reflect the views of any organization, employer, client, ministry, or affiliate.

Scripture quotations, unless otherwise noted, are taken from the King James Version of the Bible.

First Edition
10 9 8 7 6 5 4 3 2 1
Printed in the United States of America

To my family, my colleagues, my ministry partners,
and my friends who pushed me when I needed courage,
celebrated me when I reached new ground, and comforted me
when the journey was hard.

Because of you, I learned what it truly means to break forth.

Everything you were built to become
is waiting on the other side of the leader you decide to be.
BreakForth—it's time for the world to know you.

— *Nichelle L. Early*

CONTENTS

ACKNOWLEDGMENTS

First and always, to God be all the glory. Thank you for your love, your grace, your revelation, and the many gifts you have entrusted to me. Every insight in this book, and every door that has opened for me to live it, is a reflection of your faithfulness.

To my parents, **Noble and Janet White**, thank you for stewarding my upbringing with such care. Your sacrifice, your provision, and your early introduction of God into my life have shaped the woman, leader, and believer I am today. I am forever grateful that you prioritized character, faith, and excellence long before titles and accomplishments ever appeared.

To my sisters, **Tisa, Sherlyn, and Shalita**, believe it or not, many of the principles in this book were refined by watching the different leadership traits each of you carries. You have taught me about strength, resilience, compassion, perspective, and humor. And yes, some of these lessons came from the years you allowed me to "boss" you around. Thank you for loving me through all of it.

To **Michael Early and the entire Early family**, thank you for twenty-five years of love, support, and shared history. Your belief in me, even in seasons when I was still learning to believe in myself, has meant more than you know.

To my **Aunt Wanda F. Moore, Uncles Major Lang, Jay Owens, Al Harris, Jimmy Moore**; and cousins, especially **Terrance and Selena**, I love you all very much. Your encouragement, your humor, and your presence remind me that leadership is richer when it is rooted in family.

To **the teams of BreakForth Solutions, Inc.** and **BreakForth Ministries and Consulting, Inc.**, thank you for trusting me to lead. You have given me the privilege of building, stretching, and practicing many of the principles captured in these pages in real time. You have been both laboratory and legacy, and I do not take that for granted.

To the **BreakForth Solutions, Inc. "A-Team"**, thank you for standing with me in ways that go far beyond job descriptions. To **Lisa Anderson**, my CFO, who has been by my side practically since day one, your blend of financial expertise, strategic insight, and personal care has been invaluable. **Uriel Gregoire**, thank you for being the banker who not only understands the numbers, but also understands the vision. **David White** and **Jay Siembida**, your strategic financial and wealth advisory has been priceless. **Robert Burke**, your tax and accounting mastery continues to impress me. **David Black** and **Justin Banford**, thank you for your legal counsel and advocacy. And to **Lucas Aimes**, your executive operational oversight and support allow me to do what I do. I appreciate you more than words can fully express.

To **Dr. James E. Dixon** and **Nikki Dixon**, thank you for your prophetic push and unwavering encouragement. Without your challenge and your confidence, this work might still be in the realm of "one day." You helped move it into "now."

To my dear friends, **Tony and NaTosha Clemons, Vern and France Saunders, Lloyd and Tanaia Parker, Dr. Sundra Ryce, Ingrid Knight, Brian Bullock, Jermon Bafaty**, and **Jennifer Tackett**, you are each remarkable leaders in your own right. Thank you for the conversations, the courage, and the space to be both vulnerable and visionary.

To my mentor and confidant, **Dr. James Graham**, and his lovely wife, **Dr. Gloria Graham**, thank you for your pastoral covering, wise counsel, and oversight of my ministry efforts over the years. Your guidance has been a steadying force, and I love and appreciate you both more than words on a page can express.

To **Dr. Julian Dangerfield** and **Lady Lisa Dangerfield**, Chair Lady **Shamikia Ward**, and to the entire **Heritage Fellowship Church**, Reston family, thank you for your love, your support, and your confidence in the ministry and gifts God has given me.

Special thanks to **Thomasena Ellis, Markus Gaines**, and **Robert Rabinek**, for your encouragement and partnership in different seasons.

Finally, to everyone who has ever given me a leadership opportunity, opened a door, spoken a word of affirmation, challenged me to grow, or supported me in any way, thank you. Whether it was a platform, a meeting, a contract, a conversation, or a quiet prayer, you have all played a part in this journey.

I do not take lightly that you have believed in the leader I am and the leader I am still becoming. This work is, in many ways, a reflection of the deposits you have made into my life.

PREFACE

The Weight No One Warned You About

There is a particular kind of exhaustion that high-performing leaders know but rarely name. It is not the tiredness that comes from working long hours, though you have certainly logged those. It is not the pressure of a difficult quarter, a demanding client, or a team in transition, though you have navigated all of those too. It is something quieter, and far more costly. It is the weight of carrying a leadership identity that has been built almost entirely from the outside in, constructed from titles, metrics, approvals, and performance, with very little attention paid to what is happening beneath the surface.

I know that weight personally. There came a point in my leadership journey when everything I had built was real, measurable, and meaningful. The company was growing. The contracts were coming. The rooms I had worked to earn were opening. But I could not stop long enough to take any of it in. There was always another proposal due, another deliverable on the horizon, another urgency that could not wait. The wins were happening, but the celebration never was. And over time, the work that once gave me energy began to feel like a treadmill I could not step off, not because I had failed, but because the pace had consumed the very purpose it was supposed to serve. I had spent years developing the outer architecture of a leader while the inner infrastructure quietly went unattended. And the gap between the two had become unsustainable.

That reality did not arrive with a dramatic announcement. It arrived the way most leadership fractures do, gradually, then all at once. It showed up in the decisions I second-guessed longer than I should have. In the meetings where I was physically present but internally scattered. In the private moments when I asked myself whether the leader everyone else saw was actually the leader I was becoming, or simply the one I had learned to perform.

That question changed everything.

What I discovered on the other side of that season was not a new strategy. It was not a better time management system or a more sophisticated leadership model. What I found was something far more durable and far more personal, the understanding that sustainable, high-impact leadership is always an inside job. That before a leader can build an organization worth following, they must build an inner world worth leading from. That conviction, identity, resilience, clarity, legacy and execution are not soft concepts reserved for the personal development shelf. They are the load-bearing walls of everything a leader touches.

That is what this book is about.

The BreakForth Principle was written for the corporate executive who has achieved by every visible measure and still senses that something foundational is missing. It was written for the senior leader who is tired of performing at the level of their title while privately wondering whether they are operating at the depth of their calling. It was written for the woman or man who has led teams, driven results, and managed complexity, and who now stands at the intersection of what they have built and who they are still becoming, asking whether those two things are actually aligned.

This book does not offer formulas. The leaders I have led alongside, coached, and learned from do not need another framework to add to an already crowded operating model. What they need, what I needed, is permission to take the inner work as seriously as the outer work. Permission to acknowledge that burnout is not primarily a calendar problem. That leadership drift is not primarily a skills problem. That the gap between potential and impact is almost never a strategy problem. These are infrastructure problems. And infrastructure can be built.

Each chapter of this book explores one of the six pillars of what I call the BreakForth C.I.R.C.L.E., Conviction, Identity, Resilience, Clarity, Legacy, and Execution. These are not sequential steps. They are interdependent dimensions of a leader's inner world that, when developed with intention, produce the kind of stability, authority, and impact that no title alone can manufacture. You will find honest reflection in these pages, practical challenge, and the kind of direct language that high-capacity leaders deserve. I will not waste your time with vague inspiration. My commitment to you is clarity, the same clarity I had to fight for myself.

I also want you to know this: the fact that you are reading this book is not an accident. Something in you recognized that the next level of your leadership is not waiting on a bigger opportunity, a better team, or more favorable conditions. It is waiting on a more complete version of the leader you are still in the process of becoming. That recognition is not weakness. It is the beginning of everything.

You were built for more than what pressure has produced in you so far. The pages ahead are an invitation to stop managing the gap and start closing it, deliberately, structurally, and from the inside out.

It is time to BreakForth.

Nichelle L. Early

Northern Virginia
2026

INTRODUCTION

BreakForth Mindset—Why Leadership Must Begin Within

What Is the BreakForth Principle?

There comes a moment in every leader's journey when technical skills, strategic plans, and external accolades are no longer enough. A moment when performance alone cannot carry the weight of purpose. That moment is where the BreakForth Principle begins.

The BreakForth Principle is not just a framework. It is a mindset, a philosophy, and a set of internal convictions that empower leaders to rise from performance to purpose, from pressure to clarity, from burnout to breakthrough. It is the deliberate act of leading from the inside out with integrity, alignment, and a relentless commitment to becoming the kind of leader others cannot help but trust, follow, and become transformed.

Why This Principle? Why Now?

We are living in a time of constant acceleration, disruption, and distraction. Leaders are being asked to deliver more, innovate faster, and stretch further than ever before. But many are running on empty, hiding behind success, or simply going through the motions. What has been missing is not skill, ambition, or intelligence. What has been missing is alignment.

The BreakForth Principle calls leaders back to center. It dares them to confront the gaps between their outer image and their inner truth. It insists that greatness is not found in charisma, but in character. Not in noise, but in depth. Not in speed, but in discernment.

The BreakForth Mindset

To live and lead with a BreakForth Mindset means that:
- You lead from identity, not image.
- You pursue alignment before acceleration.
- You measure success by legacy, not just metrics.
- You develop a bias for internal clarity before external communication.
- You refuse to sacrifice what matters most for what looks most impressive.

This mindset does not come naturally in a world that rewards appearances and speed. It must be cultivated through intention, discipline, and courage. That is what this book is designed to help you do.

The BreakForth Model

Throughout this book, each chapter explores one of the pillars of the BreakForth Model, a set of timeless leadership principles designed to build durable, aligned, and transformative leadership. The model is not linear. It is cyclical. These principles reinforce one another and keep bringing you back to the same core question: *What kind of leader are you becoming?*

The core BreakForth Leadership Pillars form the **C.I.R.C.L.E.** that strong leaders live within:

Conviction governs your internal alignment.
Identity anchors your leadership in who you are, not just what you do.
Resilience strengthens your capacity to lead through adversity.
Clarity defines your vision and your leadership presence.
Legacy elevates your focus beyond immediate results to long-term impact.
Execution sharpens your ability to act with intention and discipline.

Together, these six pillars form a leadership CIRCLE. The more consistently you move through them, the more stable, clear, and effective your leadership becomes. You do not "check them off" once. You live in them, and you keep cycling through them as your calling and responsibilities grow.

Each chapter concludes with a highlighted BreakForth Principle that captures that chapter's core truth. These are not simply reflective thoughts. They are personal leadership codes meant to be lived, not just learned.

Let This Book Disrupt You

This book is not designed to inspire for a moment. It is designed to provoke a movement within you.

The pages ahead will not give you formulas. They will challenge your foundations. They will not offer empty motivation. They will press you into honest mastery. They will not applaud your image. They will call forth your identity.

Because the truth is, you were never meant to lead a life that is driven only by performance. You were meant to BreakForth.

Welcome to the journey.

CHAPTER 1

The Conviction Code: Leading from the Inside Out

It is one thing to wear the title of leader. It is another thing entirely to embody a leadership presence that shifts rooms, steadies teams, and changes outcomes. The world does not lack executives. It does not lack people in charge. What it lacks, desperately, is leaders who govern their inner world with the same rigor they apply to KPIs, revenue targets, and risk registers. Too many leaders can run an organization but cannot run themselves.

That is why the BreakForth Mindset begins here. Not with tactics, not with trends, not with the next leadership book. It begins with the internal authority that determines what you do when there is no applause, no certainty, and no guarantee.

Because in real leadership, the moments that shape your reputation rarely come with a warning. They arrive wrapped in pressure, ambiguity, and responsibility. A deadline shifts at the worst possible time, a client escalates a concern that feels bigger than the facts, a top performer resigns unexpectedly, a budget tightens just as demand increases, and a crisis emerges that nobody had on the risk register. In those moments, the real question is not whether you know what to do, but whether you can stay anchored enough to do it well.

Conviction Is the Quiet Strength

Conviction is not intensity. It is integrity forged under pressure. It is not about being certain of everything, but about being anchored in the few things that cannot be compromised. Conviction governs how you lead when the outcome is uncertain, when your confidence is low, when the room is silent and everyone is waiting for you to speak. It holds the line when your title is not enough and your plan is not clear.

Conviction is the quiet steel in the backbone of leaders who can be trusted. It is the internal stance that says, even if this shakes, I will not.

Conviction Defined

Conviction is the internal authority that governs how a leader thinks, decides, and stands, especially in the absence of applause, agreement, or guarantees. It is not a feeling or a preference. It is a grounded belief that has been tested by pressure, clarified by purpose, proved by consistency, and reinforced through disciplined alignment. Conviction is what remains when emotion fades and clarity is required.

In corporate life, conviction often reveals itself in places that do not look dramatic. You hear it in the moment you refuse to distort the truth just to protect the quarter. It is present when you stop granting automatic access to anyone who arrives with urgency but no clarity. Conviction is at work when you choose the right decision rather than the popular one. It is evident when you hold a standard the same way on a hard day that you do on a good day. You see it most clearly when you choose to protect the culture, even when that choice slows you down in the short term. Conviction is not a vibe. It is governance.

When You Become a Machine

Conviction begins where applause ends. It lives in the silence after the board meeting. It's in the moments when you question everything you've built. When you wonder if the sacrifices are worth it. When you scan your calendar and realize that somewhere along the line, you became a machine.

You don't notice it at first. It starts innocently enough with back-to-back meetings, then skipped lunches, then one more weekend of catching up on emails. You start saying yes because you want to be responsive, then you start saying yes because you are afraid to be inaccessible. You stop asking whether something is necessary and start asking only whether it is urgent.

Gradually your soul begins to go offline while your schedule stays online. You begin to function like an output system, not a human being. Presence gets replaced with performance. Your thoughts become bullet points. Your day becomes dictated by the next alert, the next deliverable, the next demand. You are no longer leading from vision. You are running on automation.

And the most deceptive part is that the machine version of you can still look successful from the outside. Goals continue to be met, colleagues and clients express respect, and recognition still finds its way to your inbox. Meanwhile, something very different is happening internally. There is a growing sense of detachment, a numbness that replaces true presence, a feeling of being in the room but not really connected to it. Work continues to get done, yet wholeness is missing. It resembles progress, but deep down you know something sacred in you is beginning to malfunction.

This is where many leaders lose themselves and do not realize it until their body, their relationships, or their decisions start sending signals. They call it pressure. They call it a tough season. They call it the cost of leadership. Sometimes it is none of those. Sometimes it is simply a leader who has been functioning without conviction long enough that their inner life is no longer governing their outer life.

Conviction Requires Discipline

Leadership habits are reinforced through repetition. From a neuroscience perspective, the brain adapts to what we repeatedly practice and emotionally reinforce, which is why conviction has to be trained until it becomes more than a momentary intention. Developing a disciplined relationship with conviction means more than having strong opinions or a powerful mantra. It is about forging a neural and emotional bond with the beliefs that govern your life and leadership.

Neuroscience confirms that the brain is always pattern-seeking. Without conscious reinforcement, even your best intentions are overridden by default behaviors. This is why leaders can know what is right and still do what is convenient. This is why leaders can value health and still live in crisis mode. This is why leaders can speak about boundaries and still feel guilty when they enforce them.

Conviction must be rehearsed until it becomes a reflex, not a reaction in moments of inspiration. This is where neuroplasticity matters. The brain reorganizes around what you repeat, what you emotionally reinforce, and what you practice under pressure. Without discipline, conviction remains an idea rather than a structure. It becomes an occasional motivator rather than a reliable compass.

A disciplined relationship with conviction requires deliberate conditioning. It requires that you remind your nervous system daily that you are safe to stand on what you believe. Leaders who fail in this area often confuse passion for permanence. They get stirred by a keynote, a promotion, a crisis, or a personal moment, but they are not stable enough to stay the course once comfort returns or resistance shows up. Their convictions are circumstantial, not structural.

Discipline makes conviction sustainable. Research on stress and executive functioning suggests that when leaders are under pressure, the brain can become more reactive and less deliberate, which is why disciplined patterns matter so much in high-stakes moments. That is when leaders start overreacting, overcontrolling, overcommitting, or overexplaining.

Business Implication

An unregulated leader can unintentionally create confusion, churn, and risk. They can destabilize a team with one rushed message, one reactive decision, or one inconsistent standard. This is why conviction is not inspirational. It is operational. It protects clarity, speed, and trust.

In my own leadership, conviction has had to show up most when it would have been easier to bend. I remember a moment when a client wanted us to stretch our team beyond what was healthy just to meet an unrealistic timeline. On paper, the revenue looked attractive. The opportunity seemed strategic. But the ask would have overloaded my staff, compromised quality, and undermined the very culture I had spent years building.

The easy answer would have been to say yes and figure it out later. Conviction would not allow that. After reviewing the facts and talking with my team, I went back to the client and said, "We want to support you, but not at the expense of doing poor work or burning our people out. Here is what we can commit to with excellence. If that does not work, we will step aside." They were surprised I resisted the pressure, yet they respected it. We adjusted the scope and timeline together.

That decision did more than protect one project. It sent a message internally and externally. Our standards are not for sale, even when revenue is on the line. That is what conviction looks like under pressure. It is not loud, but it is firm. It protects the long term, even when the short term is tempting.

The Gift and Temptation of Ambition

Leadership that lasts must be sustained by more than ambition. Ambition climbs. Conviction roots. Ambition pursues visibility.

Ambition, at its best, is a catalytic force. It awakens drive, sharpens focus, and pushes boundaries. It creates momentum where mediocrity would settle. Ambitious leaders often innovate, expand markets, and break barriers that others were content to tolerate. In the right hands, ambition is energy applied with direction.

But ambition also has a shadow side. When disconnected from conviction, ambition becomes performative. It begins to seek optics over outcomes and clout over clarity. The psychology of ambition reveals that while it is deeply connected to goal orientation and achievement drive, it is also susceptible to external validation loops. The brain's reward system, particularly dopaminergic pathways, responds to recognition, praise, and social proof. Over time, that feedback loop can make leaders addicted to applause and allergic to stillness.

Unchecked ambition often leads to burnout, over-identification with achievement, and emotional detachment. The more success it gains, the more it requires to feel significant. This is why some of the most publicly celebrated leaders are privately exhausted. They are running on empty but cannot stop moving because their identity has become tethered to being impressive.

Neuroscience also tells us that sustainable success requires both motivation and regulation. Ambition spikes motivation, but without the regulatory anchor of conviction, leaders operate in cycles of overdrive and crash. Conviction provides regulation. It grounds you when external rewards fade. It reminds you who you are when the crowd moves on.

Here Is the Principle

Ambition must be governed by assignment, or it will default to ego. Ambition is not the enemy. But it was never meant to lead. It is a servant, not a guide. It must report to something higher. When ambition submits to conviction, it becomes purposeful. It becomes discerning. It begins to build what lasts instead of chasing what is loud. If ambition builds the tower, conviction lays the foundation. One creates height. The other ensures it does not collapse. When ambition is fused with internal clarity, the result is not just growth. It is grounded greatness.

A Personal Foundation of Conviction

I can remember when I was younger, I was timid, shy, and soft-spoken. My father was a locomotive engineer. He drove trains for a living. And when he would wake up from working his graveyard shift, he would call me to his bedside and say, "Baby, don't ever let no one tell you what you can or cannot do. I don't care where you go, always walk tall, talk tall, and think tall."

Little did he know those words would shape who I would become. They were not words that provoked ambition. They were words that stoked a healthy conviction that I could be whoever I was wired to be. My father was not trying to make me competitive. He was trying to make me clear.

That matters, because many leaders confuse confidence with volume. My father was teaching me internal permission. He was teaching me to take up space without begging for approval. He was teaching me to lead with dignity long before I had a title that validated it.

His voice became a guidepost for the kind of leadership I now give to others. Not leadership rooted in image. Leadership anchored in identity. Leadership that understands you will eventually be required to stand alone in a decision, even if you are surrounded by people.

Conviction Is Not Optional

Conviction will strip away every excuse rooted in fear. It will not let you downplay what you carry. It will expose how you hide behind humility when it is really hesitation. Conviction will not allow you to lead for applause. It will require that you lead for impact, even if it costs you affirmation.

In practice, conviction shows up in what you tolerate. It shows up in what you postpone. It shows up in what you excuse. It shows up in whether your calendar is aligned with your values or aligned with other people's expectations. It shows up in whether you protect your peace or sell it for access.

You do not need another strategy before you settle your spirit. You do not need another mentor before you make a decision. You do not need a bigger platform. You need a stronger core. Platforms can collapse. Applause can fade. Metrics can move. But a leader whose life is governed by conviction will outlast all of it.

The Final Charge

Conviction is not convenient. It is costly. But what it gives you is far more valuable than what it requires of you. It gives you stamina. It gives you integrity. It gives you peace. And above all, it gives you freedom. Freedom to lead without pretending. Freedom to stand without shifting. Freedom to say yes and mean it, and no and not flinch.

Leadership is not about what you control. It is about what you cultivate. And nothing grows in chaos unless chaos has been normalized. Conviction reorders the internal world so that you stop repeating cycles and start establishing standards. You stop reacting and start governing.

To lead from the inside out is to decide, without apology, that your leadership will not be built on the shaky scaffolding of performance, but on the solid ground of principle. That is the only kind of leadership that truly lasts.

And here is the reason this matters for what comes next. Pressure will come. Perception will be tested. Belief will be challenged.

The BreakForth Mindset is not built for perfect seasons. It is built for real leadership in real environments, where you are required to carry weight without losing yourself.

The Conviction Standard

Conviction is not a feeling; it is a way of operating. For a BreakForth leader, conviction shows up in the choice to speak plainly when vagueness would be easier. It is present when you are willing to say no, even though a quick yes would win temporary favor.

Conviction shapes how you structure your days, aligning your calendar with your values instead of with everyone else's urgency.

It guides you to protect people and standards when no one is watching and there is no credit to be gained.

Above all, conviction keeps you from trading long-term integrity for the short-lived applause that comes from compromise.

BREAKFORTH PRINCIPLE #1:
Conviction Is Not Optional

You cannot lead beyond the strength of your internal alignment. Conviction is not optional. It is the non-negotiable infrastructure for sustainable leadership.

CHAPTER 2

Pressure Isn't the Problem, Perception Is

A Personal Moment of Pressure and Perception

I can remember when I first became the CEO of BreakForth Solutions. I had just left a role where success was supported by infrastructure. If I needed HR support, it was there. If I needed security guidance, technical expertise, contracts help, pricing insight, or administrative coordination, it was within reach. There was always a back-office team, always a system, always someone to call.

Then I sat down at my desk at BreakForth Solutions as employee number one. No back office. No safety net. No built-in layers of support. Just me, a vision, and the pressure to succeed.

The pressure was not just operational. It was personal. In that moment, I felt the weight of being an untrained CEO and the demand of meeting requirements that would determine whether this dream lived or died. It was the kind of pressure that tightens your chest and slows your thinking, not because you are incapable, but because the stakes feel immediate and final.

And my perception started talking. Not out loud to anyone else, but loud enough in my mind that it competed with my competence. I kept thinking and saying to myself, I don't know how to be a CEO. How am I going to do this? What if I fail? What if I disappoint the people who believe in me? What if I am not enough for what I just stepped into?

That was the real battle. The work was learnable. The market could be studied. The processes could be built. The true threat was what pressure was trying to convince me about myself, because perception has a way of turning temporary strain into permanent identity if you do not interrupt it. The shift came when I decided not to let pressure define me. I stopped treating pressure like a verdict and started treating it like information. I looked within and recognized I had more resourcefulness than I was giving myself credit for. I also looked around and acknowledged that support did not have to be automatic to be accessible. I could build what I needed, ask for what I did not have, learn what I had never been taught, and lead from who I was, not from who I thought a CEO was supposed to be.

That was the beginning of the BreakForth Mindset for me. Not the version you post, but the version you practice when you are alone, when the stakes are high, and when your perception is the loudest voice in the room.

Pressure is not new. What is new is the volume and velocity of pressure in modern leadership. Decisions are made faster than outcomes can be measured. The expectation to be visible, responsive, and composed has become an unspoken job requirement, especially for senior leaders. Many executives are not failing because they cannot handle responsibility. They are failing because they are absorbing pressure through an untrained lens, and their nervous system responds as if a business problem is a personal threat.

Pressure itself is neutral. It functions as a force, a demand, a weight, but it does not carry meaning on its own. Meaning is assigned by perception. The same circumstance that causes one leader to collapse can bring another leader into sharp clarity, and the distinction is not always found in the external situation. The real difference lies in the internal interpretation.

In the BreakForth Mindset, pressure is not treated as a verdict, but as data. Pressure highlights what truly matters, brings misalignment to the surface, and makes visible where systems are weak and where standards lack clarity. It does not have the power to define you unless you hand that power over, yet it will always reveal who you are in the moment. That is the point where perception becomes the hinge and determines what happens next.

Pressure as Information, Not Identity

One of the most subtle leadership traps is allowing pressure to attach itself to identity. Leaders do this in ways that sound responsible, even noble. They say, "If I don't handle this, everything will fall apart." They say, "I have to carry it, because no one else can." They say, "I cannot show weakness." Underneath those statements is an identity agreement. The leader is no longer managing a situation. The situation is managing the leader.

When pressure becomes identity, leaders become brittle. They over-control. They micromanage. They stop delegating. They stop trusting. They stop listening. They start equating fatigue with virtue. They believe exhaustion is the price of excellence, when in reality it is often the price of poor boundaries, unclear expectations, and a leader who is carrying what should have been shared.

The BreakForth Mindset rejects that agreement. Pressure is not proof that you are inadequate. Pressure is proof that something important is in motion. The question is whether you will interpret it with fear or interpret it with leadership.

The Science of Stress and the Leadership Brain

Under stress, the brain naturally shifts toward protection and threat management, which can make it harder for leaders to think with the same level of clarity, restraint, and executive control they have when they are regulated. This is useful if you are facing physical danger. It is less useful when you are facing a board meeting, a failed launch, a cyber incident, or a sudden reorganization.

In high-pressure moments, it is widely understood that the amygdala, the brain's threat detector, becomes more reactive. When the amygdala signals danger, the body releases stress hormones that increase alertness and mobilize energy. At the same time, the prefrontal cortex, the region associated with planning, inhibition, reasoning, and complex decision-making, can become less efficient. Leaders often describe this as feeling foggy, impulsive, or emotionally charged. They may be physically present, but internally they are not operating from their highest capacity.

This matters because many leadership environments reward speed. If you are not careful, you will make high-impact decisions from a stress-dominated brain state. You will confuse urgency with clarity. You will mistake reactivity for decisiveness. You will call it strategy when it is actually a stress response wearing a professional suit.

In psychology, this idea is often described as appraisal, the meaning a person assigns to what is happening. That meaning shapes attention, physiology, and behavior. If you perceive pressure as threat, your body narrows its focus, your attention becomes hyper-vigilant, and your thinking may become defensive. If you perceive pressure as challenge, your body still mobilizes energy, but your mind is more likely to stay engaged, flexible, and solution-oriented.

That is not positive thinking. That is leadership intelligence.

Perception Is the Lens That Decides Your Response

Perception is not just what you see. It is how you process what you see. It is the lens through which you interpret risk, feedback, failure, and uncertainty. Two leaders can receive the same email, read the same metrics, and sit in the same meeting, and walk away with completely different emotional responses. One becomes anxious and rigid. The other becomes calm and precise. The difference is not personality alone. The difference is perception.

Perception is shaped by experience, beliefs, and emotional memory. It is shaped by what you have survived and what you have not healed. It is shaped by the private stories you have told yourself about success, respect, safety, and control. Leaders rarely realize how much they are obeying a story until pressure exposes it.

If your internal story says, "Mistakes make me unsafe," you will lead with fear under pressure. If your internal story says, "My worth is tied to performance," you will collapse inward when outcomes are imperfect. If your internal story says, "I must prove myself," you will interpret every setback as an attack.

The BreakForth Mindset requires leaders to get honest about these internal stories. Not for self-analysis as an academic exercise, but for leadership effectiveness. An unexamined lens will sabotage your best strategy, because it will quietly distort what you believe is happening.

A Boardroom Moment: When Pressure Tries to Hijack You

I have been in rooms where the stakes were high and the temperature was higher. Financial pressure, reputational pressure, timeline pressure, performance pressure. There is a particular kind of pressure that shows up when people are waiting for you to deliver certainty in a moment where certainty is not available. As a CEO, I learned that leadership is often the art of staying grounded while others are searching for someone to absorb their anxiety.

In those moments, pressure will test your perception first. It will try to convince you that you must speak immediately, that silence equals weakness, and that slowing down equals losing control. If you accept that narrative, you will speak too soon, promise too quickly, and commit your organization to decisions that were made for emotional relief rather than strategic alignment. I had to learn to let pressure do what it does without letting it define what I do. I had to learn that composure is not personality. It is training. It is the result of practicing internal regulation long before the moment demands it.

Regulation: The Executive Skill Nobody Teaches

I can remember it like it was yesterday. My head was pounding, my chest felt tight, and it felt like my teeth and tongue were not in agreement. My words were not coming out the way I needed them to, and my eyes were getting red and blurry by the hour. I tried to push through it, because that is what high performers do when they think grit is the same thing as wisdom. But eventually I thought, I better get to my doctor, because this did not feel like normal stress anymore.

I was able to get in. My doctor looked at the numbers, looked back at me, and said, "You are experiencing stage 2 hypertension. Whatever is going on in your outside world is severely impacting your internal world. We must regulate your blood pressure immediately."

That word hit me harder than the diagnosis, because it named what I had been avoiding. Regulate. Not just my blood pressure, but my internal state. Not just my health, but my leadership pattern. In that moment, I realized something that every executive eventually learns, either through maturity or through pain. If you do not regulate your internal state, the role will regulate you, and it will not do it gently.

Pressure will start showing up in your body, your sleep, your relationships, and your decision-making. It will cloud your thinking. It will shorten your patience. It will train you to live in urgency until urgency feels normal. I walked out of that appointment with a commitment that was bigger than medication. I knew I needed to regulate my reactions to what showed up in my day, or I was not going to survive the job of CEO with my health, clarity, and leadership integrity intact.

That was the beginning of a more disciplined leadership life. I began to build principles that forced me to slow down. I became more intentional about accessibility. I stopped rewarding reactivity. I learned how to pause long enough to hear myself think. I stopped letting other people's urgency become my emergency. An unregulated leader can unintentionally create risk, confusion, and churn, and the damage rarely shows up immediately. It shows up later in misalignment, attrition, rework, and mistrust.

Most leadership development programs focus on communication, influence, and strategy. Those are essential. But one of the most valuable executive skills is regulation, the ability to manage your internal state under pressure so you can lead from clarity instead of adrenaline.

Regulation means you can feel stress without becoming reckless. It means you can experience fear without surrendering to it. It means you can hear criticism without needing to defend your ego. It means you can take in complex information without rushing to a conclusion that you will later need to undo.

Regulation is not denial. It is leadership maturity, and it is one of the fastest ways to change your leadership outcomes without changing your title.

One practical way to think about regulation is this: under pressure, your attention narrows. You start scanning for what could go wrong. Your brain is trying to protect you, but it can also trap you. Leaders with a BreakForth Mindset learn to widen attention intentionally. They slow down enough to separate facts from assumptions, signals from noise, and urgency from importance.

This is where discipline becomes spiritual and strategic at the same time. Discipline is what allows you to pause without freezing, to think without spiraling, and to respond without reacting.

The Perception Trap: When Leaders Confuse Noise for Truth

Pressure often arrives with noise. Opinions, forecasts, worst-case scenarios, heated messages, social media, internal politics, and external expectations. Noise is not always false, but it is often unfiltered. It is often emotional. It is often designed to transfer anxiety from one person to another.

Leaders who do not guard perception start internalizing noise as truth. They allow other people's fear to become their own. They allow incomplete information to become a conclusion. They allow urgency to become identity. And when urgency becomes identity, leaders start making decisions to feel relief, not to produce results.

In the BreakForth Mindset, leaders practice three separations, not as theory, but as discipline.

> **First**, separating facts from stories. Facts are what can be observed and verified. Stories are the interpretation layered on top, and stories tend to get dramatic under pressure.

Second, separating urgency from importance. Urgency is the clock. Importance is the consequence. Everything loud is not important, and everything important is not loud.

Third, separating responsibility from ownership. You can be responsible without carrying what is not yours to carry, and you can lead accountability without absorbing anxiety.

Those separations sound simple. They are not. They require internal discipline and emotional maturity, and they require leaders to stop being impressed by intensity.

There was a time when a senior manager at a client site misread a situation in a way that almost damaged a strong relationship. A minor delay in deliverables triggered an internal email storm. By the time the message reached me, the narrative had shifted from "we missed a date" to "this vendor cannot be trusted."

The facts did not support that story. The delay had a clear cause, it had been communicated, and recovery steps were in place. The perception trap took hold because one leader allowed internal pressure to color their interpretation. They sent messages from frustration instead of from facts.

We reset the conversation by walking through what actually happened, what had been assumed, and what had been said. Once perception was corrected, the tone changed. We did not just salvage the relationship. We strengthened it because we proved we could handle tension with clarity rather than with blame.

Perception traps work like that. They turn small issues into big stories. The story becomes more dangerous than the issue.

Leaders who learn to slow down, verify, and reframe protect the business from paying for a story that never should have been written.

Why Perception Becomes a Culture Issue

Perception is not just personal. It becomes cultural.

If leaders perceive pressure as threat, they will build cultures driven by fear. Communication becomes guarded. Innovation becomes risky. People become more concerned with being safe than being excellent. Over time, the organization becomes reactive, and reactivity becomes normalized. The business pays for it through slow execution, talent loss, and teams that stop telling the truth early.

If leaders perceive pressure as challenge and information, they build cultures that learn. Communication becomes clearer. Accountability becomes healthier. People become more committed to solutions than to blame. Over time, the organization becomes resilient, and resilience becomes a competitive advantage. Culture reflects how leaders actually see and respond to pressure. Over time, the way leadership perceives and behaves becomes the pattern the organization unconsciously follows.

This is why the BreakForth Mindset is not a personal pep talk. It is an executive operating system. It is how leaders learn to lead themselves so they can lead others well.

Reframing Without Pretending

Some leaders hear "perception" and assume it means pretending everything is fine. That is not the BreakForth Mindset. Reframing is not denial. Reframing is precision. Reframing means you look at reality and ask better questions, because better questions produce better leadership.

Instead of asking, "Why is this happening to me?" you ask, "What is this revealing about our systems?"

Instead of asking, "What if I fail?" you ask, "What does excellence require from me in this moment?"

Instead of asking, "How do I control this?" you ask, "What do I need to stabilize first?"

Better questions create better perception. Better perception creates better leadership.

Faith, Perception, and the Inner Agreements Leaders Make

If you are a faith-rooted leader, perception carries an additional layer. You are not only interpreting pressure through experience and training. You are interpreting it through belief.

Many leaders say they trust God, but their perception under pressure reveals what they truly believe. If your internal agreement is that everything depends on you, pressure will become crushing. If your internal agreement is that your purpose is real and you are not alone in carrying it, pressure can become heavy, but it will not become defining.

Faith does not remove pressure. Faith reshapes perception. Faith keeps you from confusing a difficult season with a failed assignment. Faith keeps you from interpreting resistance as rejection. Faith keeps you anchored when outcomes are delayed.

In practical terms, faith-based perception means you remain honest about what is happening while refusing to catastrophize. It means you can hold urgency without panic. It means you can lead with conviction without needing to control every variable.

This is not spirituality as decoration. This is spirituality as leadership stability.

The BreakForth Protocol for Pressure

A BreakForth Mindset leader does not wait until pressure spikes to learn how to respond. They build protocols, because pressure loves leaders who improvise. Here is a simple protocol that has helped me and many leaders I coach. It is not a script. It is an internal sequence.

First, name the pressure without exaggeration. Speak it in plain language. "We missed the milestone." "The client is dissatisfied." "The revenue forecast shifted." "The team is fragmented."

Second, locate what you are feeling without letting it lead. "I feel disappointed." "I feel concerned." "I feel stretched." "I feel the urge to fix this immediately."

Third, return to facts. What is verified. What is unknown. What is assumed.

Fourth, choose the next right action, not the perfect action. Pressure tries to push leaders into dramatic moves. Mature leaders make precise moves.

Fifth, communicate from clarity, not adrenaline. If you speak while flooded, you will often create additional pressure through your words, because your tone will transmit what your mind is carrying.

This protocol sounds simple because it is. The power is in consistency.

A 60-Second Pressure Reset

Before you walk into a high-stakes meeting, give yourself sixty seconds to reset. Quietly ask:

1. What is actually happening, without drama?
2. What am I feeling, and what do I want to do with that feeling?
3. What outcome would excellence require from me in this room?

Then decide one thing: "What is the most important tone I need to set, and what is the clearest message I must leave behind." That brief reset can be the difference between leading from reaction and leading from perception.

When Perception Shifts, Performance Shifts

Leaders often try to solve pressure with more activity. More meetings. More emails. More monitoring. More control. The BreakForth Mindset teaches a different order. Change perception first. Then performance will follow.

When perception changes, your physiology changes. When physiology changes, your attention changes. When attention changes, your decisions change. When decisions change, your outcomes change. This is why perception is leadership, and why perception is not soft.

If you want to lead at a higher level, your mind cannot be trained only for execution. It must be trained for interpretation. It must be trained to read pressure accurately, and not to confuse volume with truth.

Pressure is not the problem. Pressure is the environment. Perception is the hinge.

If you want your leadership to last, you will have to become the kind of leader who can hold pressure without becoming pressured. Not numb. Not detached. Not in denial. Grounded. Clear. Disciplined. Governed.

That is what the BreakForth Mindset produces. It does not remove the demands of leadership. It builds leaders who can carry those demands without losing themselves.

There is a reason seasoned leaders are described as steady. Steadiness is not personality, and it is not luck. It is the outcome of disciplined perception. It is the ability to stay anchored to facts, values, and next actions when everyone else is being pulled toward panic, blame, or noise. When you change your lens, you change what you notice. When you change what you notice, you change how you lead.

That is why perception is not a soft skill. It is a business advantage.

BREAKFORTH PRINCIPLE #2:
Perception Governs Performance

Pressure does not decide your leadership outcome. Your perception does. Train your lens, regulate your internal state, and lead from clarity, not threat.

CHAPTER 3

Break the Lid: The Neuroscience of Belief

There is a ceiling most leaders never see. It is not visible on an org chart. It does not appear in a budget forecast. It is not listed among risks in a program plan. Yet it quietly shapes how far a leader will go, how boldly they will decide, and how much influence they will allow themselves to carry. That ceiling is belief.

Belief is not the same as optimism, and it is not wishful thinking. Belief is the internal model you use to interpret reality. It shapes what you notice, what you ignore, what you tolerate, and what you attempt. It influences what you consider possible, what you assume will fail, and what you feel you have the right to pursue. Belief functions like a leadership operating system, running in the background of every strategic decision and every difficult conversation, often without your permission and sometimes without your awareness.

The corporate world tends to treat belief like a soft topic, a personal matter, something you keep private. That is a mistake. Belief is not soft. Belief is structural. It shapes performance because it shapes perception, and perception shapes choices. Leaders talk about transformation, innovation, and resilience, but many are trying to execute a vision that their belief system quietly rejects. You cannot sustain a future you do not believe you can carry.

I can remember sitting at my desk early on, letting myself say the dream out loud. One day, BreakForth is going to reach ten million in revenue. The words felt bold, and they also felt expensive. Almost immediately, my inner critic answered back with a tone that sounded like caution, but carried the weight of fear. Who have you ever seen in your life that has accomplished that. Don't jump out there too far, because if something happens, you could lose everything.

And it was not just fear of failure. It was fear of what success would say about me, and fear of what people would accuse me of once I started reaching for more.

A former supervisor had once accused me of never being satisfied with my present success. Those words haunted me because they sounded spiritual. They sounded like a character issue. They sounded like the kind of critique you are supposed to accept quietly and correct. At the time, we had just won our first four-million-dollar contract, and part of my belief system acquiesced. I started questioning whether wanting more meant I was ungrateful. I started confusing hunger with arrogance. I started interpreting vision as dissatisfaction.

That is how belief ceilings work. They rarely announce themselves as limitation. They present themselves as maturity, humility, or realism. They try to keep you safe by keeping you small. That is when companies plateau, not because the market is closed, but because the leader's belief is. The closure quietly shows up in conservative decisions, delayed bets, talent underutilization, and strategies that protect comfort more than they pursue growth.

But something in me would not let the dream die. I remembered what my father used to tell me when I was younger, to walk tall, talk tall, and think tall. I realized he was not teaching ambition. He was teaching internal permission. He was teaching conviction. And in that moment, I made a decision. I would not treat a bigger vision as a betrayal of gratitude. I would treat it as an assignment that required capacity.

So I began to condition my spirit, my mind, and my perception to see beyond right now. I did it through repeated thoughts, repeated emotions, repeated visions, and repeated behaviors that forecasted where I desired the company to go. I built language around growth that did not dishonor what we had already achieved. I practiced seeing ten million without despising four million. I practiced thanking God for what was present while still stretching toward what was possible. As my internal capacity expanded, our business began to expand with it. The growth was not only the result of strategy. It was the result of belief making room for what leadership required. That is the part people do not always see. Before revenue grows, you grow. Before systems scale, your belief system has to scale. Before the organization can carry more, the leader has to believe they can carry more, and then live in a way that proves it.

In the BreakForth Mindset, belief is not a motivational accessory. It is a measurable, trainable, and strategic asset. It is also a liability when it is left unmanaged. When leaders are under pressure, they do not rise to the level of their ambition. They fall to the level of their conditioning. Conditioning is built by repeated thoughts, repeated emotional states, and repeated behaviors. That is why belief deserves executive attention.

Belief Is a Prediction System

One of the most useful ways to understand belief is to treat it as prediction. The brain is not merely a passive receiver of information. It is an active forecaster. It constantly anticipates what is about to happen and prepares the body and mind accordingly. Your brain is always asking, consciously or not, what does this mean for me, and what should I do next.

Beliefs are the templates the brain uses to answer those questions quickly. If your belief is that conflict is dangerous, you will avoid difficult conversations, even when you are capable of handling them. If your belief is that you must be perfect to be respected, you will over-prepare, over-control, and often under-delegate. If your belief is that you are only valuable when you are producing, you will ignore rest and call it discipline. In each case, belief is not just a thought. It is a prediction that shapes behavior.

From a neuroscience perspective, this matters because predictions influence attention. Attention is selective. The brain filters reality because it cannot take in everything. It prioritizes what it believes matters. That is why two leaders can sit in the same meeting and walk away with different conclusions. Their beliefs filtered what they noticed and how they interpreted it.

Leaders often believe they are being objective. Many are not. Many are being consistent with their internal model, and calling it judgment.

Why High Performers Still Feel Stuck

It is common to find leaders who are highly competent but internally capped. They are respected. They are capable. They deliver results. Yet they feel a quiet tension, as if their life and leadership are running below potential. They cannot always explain it, but they feel it. That is often a belief ceiling operating beneath a polished exterior.

A belief ceiling can sound like professionalism. I am just being realistic. That is not how things work here. I do not want to rock the boat. We have tried that before. I am not sure I am the right person for that. I need more experience. This is not the right time.

Those statements can be wise in certain contexts. The problem is when they become default language. When they are not conclusions based on data, but reflexes based on fear. When they are not discernment, but self-protection. Leaders often call it strategy. Sometimes it is simply a belief that has not been challenged.

I worked with a Vice President who had a stellar track record and a team that trusted them. On paper, everything looked impressive. Yet every time a new, visible opportunity surfaced, they found a way to step back. "This is not the right time." "I think someone else should lead this." "I am not sure the organization is ready."

At first, it sounded like wisdom. After a while, the pattern became clear. Their belief system had drawn an invisible line around their own influence. Anything beyond that line felt unsafe. They called it timing. It was really a belief lid.

Once we named it, we could challenge it. The moment they agreed to lead one of those higher-stakes initiatives, with support and structure, they stepped into a level of impact that had been waiting on them for years. The organization had not been blocking them. Their belief had.

Self-Efficacy and Executive Capacity

Psychology offers a well-established idea that maps closely to what leaders experience, the belief that you can execute the actions necessary to produce a result. It is not arrogance. It is not entitlement. It is confidence grounded in capability and learning.

When self-efficacy is strong, leaders persist longer, recover faster from setbacks, and take on challenges with more skillful energy. When self-efficacy is weak, leaders avoid challenges, interpret setbacks as personal failure, and become risk-averse. They may still perform, but they perform within a narrower range, and that narrowing eventually becomes noticeable in decision quality and leadership presence.

In executive environments, the consequences are significant. Weak self-efficacy often shows up as delayed decisions, excessive approvals, unclear accountability, and an over-reliance on consensus. It can also show up as perfectionism disguised as excellence. Leaders keep refining instead of releasing. They keep analyzing instead of acting.

Strong self-efficacy does not eliminate mistakes. It changes the meaning of mistakes.

Leaders stop treating mistakes as shame and start treating them as feedback. That shift changes everything because shame collapses learning. Shame turns a misstep into a personal indictment. It makes leaders hide, over-explain, or become defensive. It makes teams cautious, because people can feel when mistakes are punished emotionally, even if they are tolerated verbally. In a shame-driven environment, people do not bring problems forward early. They soften the truth. They avoid ownership. They wait until something becomes unavoidable, then it becomes expensive.

Feedback does the opposite. Feedback keeps the mistake in its proper category. It says, this happened, it matters, and we can learn from it, without turning it into a character judgment. Leaders who treat mistakes as feedback stay oriented toward improvement rather than image management. They ask better questions. What failed, exactly. What did we assume. What did we not see. What would we do differently next time. What does this reveal about the system, the communication, the timeline, or the decision process. Those questions move a team from embarrassment to execution.

This is where belief is revealed. If a leader believes mistakes equal incompetence, they will lead with fear and control. If a leader believes mistakes are part of mastery, they will lead with clarity and accountability. The difference is not permissiveness. It is maturity. Leaders who treat mistakes as feedback do not lower standards. They increase learning speed. They create an environment where problems are surfaced earlier, decisions improve faster, and trust grows because truth is safe enough to be spoken.

When you shift mistakes from shame to feedback, you protect three things every organization depends on: transparency, innovation, and momentum.

How Belief Becomes Biology

Belief is not just mental. It becomes physical, and it shows up in the leader's presence before it ever shows up in the numbers.

When a leader believes a situation is unsafe, the body prepares for threat. Stress hormones rise. Attention narrows. The mind becomes more defensive. Tone changes. Patience shortens. That leader may think they are being direct, but what the room feels is urgency and tension.

When a leader believes a situation is challenging but manageable, the body mobilizes energy without collapsing into panic. The leader stays more present. They can listen. They can ask better questions. They can separate what is urgent from what is important. They can regulate.

This is why belief is not private. Belief is contagious. It shapes the emotional climate of a team. Leaders do not simply communicate information. They transmit state. They transmit confidence or anxiety, clarity or confusion, steadiness or volatility.

Executives often ask, how do I improve culture. One answer is to improve belief. Not slogans. Not posters. Not surface-level messaging. Belief in what is possible. Belief in the team's capacity. Belief in accountability without shame. Belief in learning instead of blame. Culture follows belief.

The Lid You Did Not Choose

Some belief ceilings are inherited. They come from childhood messages, early career experiences, or environments where punishment was attached to risk. Some belief ceilings come from identity and representation. They come from being the first, the only, or the youngest in the room. They come from feeling you must perform twice as well to receive half the credibility. Some belief ceilings come from failure. A leader tries something bold, it does not work, and their brain builds a protective story, do not do that again.

There is nothing wrong with learning from experience. The issue is when the protective story becomes a prison. A leader may not realize they are leading from a lid. They just know they feel cautious. They feel hesitant. They feel like they cannot fully exhale. They might blame the market, the team, or the timing. Sometimes it is none of those. Sometimes it is a belief ceiling that has never been named.

The BreakForth Mindset teaches leaders to do something many avoid, interrogate the invisible. What belief is governing you right now. Not what you say you believe, but what you consistently act as if is true.

Belief, Faith, and Integrity

For faith-rooted leaders, belief carries an additional layer. Faith is not an emotional surge. Faith is not denial. Faith is a disciplined trust that shapes perception and choices under pressure. Faith does not ignore facts. Faith refuses to be ruled by fear.

Some leaders separate faith from corporate life as if faith is only for personal hardship. Yet corporate leadership is filled with hardship. Decisions affect people's livelihoods. Market shifts can destabilize plans overnight. Crisis can arrive without warning. If faith does not stabilize your inner life in these moments, then faith has been reduced to inspiration instead of leadership strength.

The BreakForth Mindset does not ask leaders to use spirituality as decoration. It treats faith as internal alignment. Faith, when mature, strengthens conviction. It keeps you from outsourcing your identity to outcomes. It keeps you from interpreting a difficult season as a personal failure. It keeps you steady when the metrics are not.

Faith does not remove the lid automatically. It teaches you to challenge it with discipline, clarity, and integrity.

The Brain's Attention System and What You Notice

There is a practical reason belief matters. Belief changes what you see.

The brain's attention system filters information constantly. In practical terms, people tend to notice what matches what they already expect, value, or fear. That is why belief changes not only what you think, but what you see and respond to.

If you believe your organization cannot change, you will notice every example that confirms stagnation. If you believe people are not trustworthy, you will notice every mistake and interpret it as character. If you believe you are behind, you will notice every competitor's success and interpret it as evidence of your inadequacy.

Belief does not just filter reality. It frames it. This is why leaders can be presented with opportunity and still respond with hesitation. Their belief system did not register opportunity. It registered risk. Breaking the lid means training the lens so opportunity is not dismissed as danger.

Breaking the Lid Without Becoming Delusional

Some leaders hear belief and assume it means ignoring limitations or pretending the numbers do not matter. That is not what mature belief looks like.

Mature belief is grounded. It acknowledges reality while refusing to be imprisoned by it. It does not claim certainty where there is none. It claims responsibility where there is.

A BreakForth Mindset leader does not say, everything will work out. They say, we will do the work, we will learn quickly, we will tell the truth, and we will make disciplined decisions. They do not assume the path will be easy. They assume they can adapt, and they build systems that support adaptation. This is a more powerful belief than perfection. It is the belief that you can respond well.

Belief in the Boardroom

Belief shows up in how leaders handle risk. It shows up in whether they empower teams or hoard control. It shows up in whether they give honest feedback or avoid tension. It shows up in whether they build leaders or build dependency.

A senior executive I worked with once led a highly capable team, but you would never know it by the way decisions moved. Everything slowed down at the top. People called it thoroughness. The leader called it quality control. But the team experienced it as hesitation wrapped in process. Every recommendation required one more review. Every proposal needed one more meeting. Every risk needed one more layer of protection.

When we got honest, the real issue was not competence, it was belief. The leader did not fully believe the team could carry ownership without creating a mess that would reflect back on them. So they held the steering wheel tight, not because they loved control, but because they feared consequences. And that belief shaped the whole organization. Talented people stopped taking initiative because they already knew it would be overridden. High performers stopped offering bold ideas because they did not want to spend a week defending them. Eventually, the leader got what they feared most. The best talent disengaged, speed collapsed, and the organization became safe in the way that keeps you employed, but not in the way that keeps you competitive.

Belief always shows up in throughput. When belief is low, decisions become expensive, approvals multiply, and speed becomes the first casualty. When belief is mature, leaders delegate with clarity, hold standards without drama, and create environments where accountability feels stabilizing, not threatening.

When leaders have a low belief in others, they over-approve and over-review. When leaders have a low belief in themselves, they seek constant validation and prefer consensus because it spreads responsibility. When leaders have mature belief, they can take responsibility without dramatizing it. They can set standards without shaming people. They can take risks without gambling. They can be decisive without being reckless. Mature belief produces mature leadership.

A BreakForth Practice: Belief Audits

Belief will not change because you read a chapter. It changes through awareness and repetition. A belief audit is a disciplined practice of identifying the beliefs that are driving your leadership. The goal is not self-criticism. The goal is clarity.

Start with three prompts. First, what do you repeatedly avoid. Second, what do you repeatedly over-control. Third, what do you repeatedly tolerate that conflicts with your stated standards. Those three areas often reveal your active belief system.

Here is what I call the Belief Lid Signals. These are patterns I see in smart leaders who are operating below their real capacity, even while appearing successful on paper.

- You keep asking for one more data point, not because you need clarity, but because you want cover.
- You call it excellence, but it is really control, and it is costing your team speed and confidence.
- You avoid one hard conversation, then you end up in five meetings trying to manage the symptoms.
- You delay decisions until they become emergencies, then you call the emergency leadership pressure.
- You over-function in areas your team should own, then you wonder why they are not growing.
- You tolerate what you privately disagree with, then you label your discomfort as stress instead of misalignment.
- You keep your vision small enough to feel safe, then you tell yourself you are being realistic.

If any of these feel familiar, it is not condemnation. It is information. A belief lid does not mean you are weak. It means something in you is trying to protect you, and protection is often where progress goes to die.

If you avoid confrontation, you may believe conflict will damage relationships. If you over-control execution, you may believe people cannot be trusted, or you may believe mistakes will reflect on you. If you tolerate misalignment, you may believe addressing it will cost you approval. Once a belief is named, it can be challenged.

A BreakForth Mindset leader replaces vague beliefs with disciplined statements.

> Not, I hope this works.
> But, we are capable of learning faster than the problem is changing.

> Not, I am not ready.
> But, I will be ready through action, feedback, and disciplined improvement.

> Not, I cannot handle this.
> But, I can handle what is mine to handle, and I will build support for what requires a team.

The replacement is not a slogan. It is a leadership agreement. I also recommend adopting executive agreements that your leadership team can live by. These are not motivational statements. These are operating commitments that protect speed, trust, and accountability.

- We will not confuse caution with strategy. If we are hesitating, we will name what we are protecting and decide with clarity.
- We will tell the truth early, because late truth is expensive. We will surface issues while they are still solvable.
- We will move with discipline. We will make reversible decisions faster, and we will make irreversible decisions with clarity and ownership.

When a leader repeats these agreements long enough, they stop being words. They become culture.

Belief does not disappear just because you notice it. It must be replaced. Replacement happens through disciplined agreements that are lived, not recited. A leader who once believed, "I am not ready," begins to live as if, "I will get ready through action and feedback, not endless preparation." A leader who once believed, "If I do not control everything, everything will fall apart," begins to operate from, "My job is to build systems and leaders, not to be the system." A leader who once believed, "Speaking up will cost me," replaces it with, "Silence will cost more, because it will cost my integrity." Those replacement agreements become the new scripts that guide decisions when pressure tests old patterns.

The Role of Repetition and Emotional Weight

Beliefs are strengthened by repetition and emotional weight. The brain learns through frequency and intensity. If a leader repeatedly tells themselves a fearful story in high-stress moments, that story becomes more accessible and more believable over time.

The opposite is also true. When leaders practice disciplined interpretation under stress, they build new pathways. They become more capable of clarity in future pressure. This is why regulation and belief are connected. If you cannot regulate your internal state, you cannot access your best thinking. If you cannot access your best thinking, you cannot challenge the lid.

Breaking the lid requires both belief and discipline.

When Belief Shifts, Leadership Expands

Belief is the ceiling that determines how much capacity you will allow yourself to hold. When belief shifts, leaders become more present. They become more decisive. They become more generous with delegation. They stop confusing control with responsibility, and they stop confusing pace with panic. They also become more honest. Leaders with mature belief tell the truth sooner. They do not hide bad news until it becomes a crisis. They do not pretend to know what they do not know. They do not posture. They lead.

That is what makes belief an executive asset. It increases speed. It increases trust. It increases learning. It reduces noise. It reduces churn. A leader who breaks the lid does not become loud. They become clear. They stop asking for permission to operate in the fullness of their assignment. They stop shrinking their vision to match other people's comfort. They lead as if alignment matters more than approval, because it does.

That is the BreakForth Mindset.

BREAKFORTH PRINCIPLE #3:
Belief Sets the Ceiling

Your leadership expands to the level of belief you are willing to discipline. Break the lid by training your lens, strengthening self-efficacy, and choosing grounded courage over protective hesitation.

CHAPTER 4

Built to BreakForth: Architecting Your Inner World

Leadership can look strong on the outside and still feel unstable on the inside. Many executives carry significant responsibility with competence, yet experience a private fatigue that does not match the "successful" picture others see. That fatigue is not always a workload problem. Often it is a systems problem, and the system is internal.

External outcomes remain stable only as long as internal structure can support them. Most leaders were trained to produce results, not to build the inner framework that makes those results sustainable. Promotions often reward execution. The role later demands regulation. That gap is where many leaders lose clarity, peace, and consistency.

The BreakForth Mindset is not only about breaking through external barriers. It is about building the inner architecture that can carry pressure, growth, and complexity without draining the leader or destabilizing the organization. The question is not whether you can do more. The question is whether your inner world can carry more without becoming noisy, reactive, or depleted.

Conviction, perception, and belief are raw materials. This chapter focuses on structure. Structure is what turns those materials into a leadership system that holds.

Inner Architecture Is Leadership Infrastructure

In corporate environments, leaders understand infrastructure. Systems, frameworks, governance, and the reality that a business can only scale as fast as its foundation can support. When infrastructure is weak, growth becomes chaotic. Revenue can rise while culture breaks. Headcount can increase while performance slips. Leaders know what happens when business systems are underbuilt.

The same principle applies internally. Responsibility can expand while clarity shrinks. Visibility can increase while peace disappears. Influence can grow while emotional steadiness erodes. When internal infrastructure is weak, leadership becomes reactive, inconsistent, and expensive. Decision quality declines. Communication becomes fragmented. Teams hesitate because support feels unpredictable. Trust erodes through repeated instability that people feel even when nobody names it.

I learned this in a way that was painfully honest.

I can remember having a meeting with my executive coach during a season when, from the outside, things looked like they were going exactly the way they were supposed to go. We were building credibility. The company was gaining notoriety. We were winning awards. We were meeting people we needed to meet and getting in rooms that used to feel out of reach.

But I told her something I had not said out loud to many people. I said, "I feel like I'm following all the rules. I'm doing all the right things and going to all the right places. But I still don't have clarity or peace about where I'm leading this company." Then I said what was really underneath it. "I feel empty. I feel alone. I cannot explain it, but something on the inside is missing."

She listened, then said something that cut through the noise in one sentence. "You are investing so much in the company's infrastructure and where it is going. What are you investing in yourself."

That question exposed what I had normalized. Systems, plans, partnerships, and performance were being built, while the leader carrying it all was being neglected. Promises to exercise, eat well, rest, take vitamins, take an actual day off, or do something restorative kept getting broken in the name of business objectives that felt more urgent. The choice felt responsible in the moment. The long-term cost was hidden.

Every broken promise to self weakened internal infrastructure. It trained the body to accept depletion as normal. It trained the mind to live in urgency. It reduced capacity without announcing that it was happening. The impact showed up in how I interpreted situations, how quickly I got irritated, and how hard it felt to stay steady when pressure hit. Fatigue distorts perception. Depletion invites reactivity. Unaddressed strain makes small problems feel personal. That conversation became a leadership standard for me. It is possible to build a strong company and still become an unstable leader if the inner world is underbuilt. And when a leader's internal infrastructure is weak, the business eventually feels it, even if the numbers look good for a while.

Organizations do not only scale through strategy. They scale through the leader's capacity to carry complexity without losing clarity, stability, or self.

Inner architecture is the set of internal systems that govern how you think, interpret, decide, communicate, recover, and lead under pressure. It includes standards, boundaries, self-talk, emotional regulation, and the ability to tell the truth early. When those internal systems are strong, leadership becomes steadier and teams become faster. When those systems are weak, leadership becomes noisier and execution slows.

A leader with strong inner architecture does not just look stable. Stability becomes operational. It affects decision velocity, risk management, and the organization's ability to execute without confusion. It determines whether issues get surfaced early or hidden until they are expensive.

The Hidden Reason Leaders Burn Out

Burnout is often framed as too much work. Sometimes that is true. More often, burnout is the result of internal strain that never gets addressed. Unchecked assumptions. Unprocessed emotions. A calendar that never breathes. Decision-making that happens under adrenaline. Leadership that stays "on" so consistently that recovery starts to feel like irresponsibility. Workload is visible. Internal noise is quieter, but it is just as costly.

Many leaders ask for a better strategy when what is needed is a better structure. Without internal structure, even good leadership habits turn into pressure multipliers. Responsiveness becomes over-responsiveness. Accessibility turns into constant interruption. High standards slip into perfectionism. Care for others becomes self-neglect. And before long, the leader is carrying an organization while privately losing clarity, patience, and peace.

A familiar pattern follows. More effort is applied to feel safer. More availability is offered to feel more in control. More responsibility is taken on to avoid disappointment. More communication is added to prevent misunderstandings. More over-functioning shows up to reduce the risk of failure. The activity looks like leadership. The results often feel like exhaustion. The BreakForth Mindset teaches a different order. Leadership is not sustained by force. It is sustained by alignment. Alignment requires internal design, not just external output. When internal design is missing, leadership becomes reactive. When leadership becomes reactive, stress becomes constant. When stress becomes constant, the body and mind start sending signals that can no longer be ignored. Burnout is not always a sign that the leader cannot handle the role. Sometimes it is a sign that the role has outgrown the leader's internal infrastructure. The answer is not always doing less. The answer is building better.

I have seen leaders transform their inner world in ninety days when they treat inner architecture as seriously as they treat revenue. One executive went from constant email at midnight, back-to-back meetings, and constant escalation, to a calendar with protected thinking blocks, defined office hours, and clearer delegation. At the beginning, they described feeling "foggy and short-fused." Ninety days later, they described feeling "clearer, more patient, and less reactive."

Nothing magical happened. They enforced a few standards, honored a recovery rhythm, and stopped saying yes to everything. The team noticed. The tone changed. Decision quality improved. That is what internal architecture does. It does not remove pressure, but it gives pressure a stable container.

A Corporate Vignette: When the Leader Becomes the Bottleneck

A senior leader once told me, "I don't understand why my team is not moving faster. We have the talent. We have the budget. We have the strategy." On paper, that was true. In practice, the team was cautious. Decisions slowed down. People kept asking for approvals. The leader felt constantly interrupted.

A few conversations revealed the pattern. The leader was quick to correct, quick to rewrite, and quick to jump in. That approach was rooted in care and high standards, but it sent an unintended message: initiative is risky here. People adapted. They stopped moving without permission. They stopped proposing bold ideas unless they could fully defend them. They started escalating everything early to avoid being corrected later. The leader became frustrated and worked harder. More reviews. More check-ins. More oversight. The team moved slower.

The leader felt more pressure. That feedback loop is common, and it rarely gets labeled correctly. This was not a talent problem. It was an internal architecture problem. The leader's internal system had learned that control equals safety. That belief shaped behavior. That behavior shaped culture. That culture reduced speed. The goal is not for leaders to become hands-off.

The goal is to build internal structure that supports delegation, clarity, and calm authority, even when stakes are high.

The Four Rooms of the Inner World

Architecting the inner world starts with naming what needs to be built. Think of the inner world as a leadership headquarters with four rooms that require maintenance and discipline.

Room One: The Mind The mind is where thoughts, assumptions, and narratives form. Under pressure, the mind can exaggerate risk, predict rejection, or interpret uncertainty as threat. A leader does not need perfect thinking. A leader needs disciplined thinking. Thinking anchored in facts, aligned with conviction, and trained to reject fear-driven conclusions. *A practical standard is simple: facts first, interpretation second, reaction last.*

Room Two: The Nervous System The nervous system determines whether pressure gets interpreted as information or threat. It influences tone, pacing, patience, and decision speed. Leaders who cannot regulate often communicate too fast, decide too quickly, or avoid decisions altogether. The issue is not intelligence. The issue is internal state. *Regulation is not wellness. It is executive function.*

Room Three: The Spirit For faith-rooted leaders, spiritual grounding is not separate from leadership. It stabilizes identity, sustains conviction, and guards against becoming performance-driven. When spiritual grounding weakens, outcomes start carrying too much emotional weight. Leaders become unstable when metrics move. Anxiety rises. Discernment slips. *Spiritual grounding is the room that keeps leadership honest.*

Room Four: The Standards Standards are where boundaries and non-negotiables live. Standards protect capacity. When standards are vague, everything becomes negotiable. When everything becomes negotiable, exhaustion becomes predictable. Standards are not rigidity. *Standards are stewardship.*

Default Architecture and Why It Limits Leaders

Many leaders never build inner architecture intentionally. The inner world gets built by default. Childhood messages. Workplace survival strategies. Trauma. Expectations. High-performance habits that worked in one season and became unhealthy in another.

Default architecture often includes over-functioning, hyper-accessibility, people-pleasing, perfectionism, control, constant motion, and conflict avoidance. These patterns are not always character flaws. Often they are coping mechanisms. Coping mechanisms that never get updated become constraints.

Internal architecture debt accumulates quietly. It grows every time you say yes when you should pause, break a boundary you promised to keep, ignore a health signal, or avoid a conversation your spirit knows you need to have. For a while, nothing obvious breaks. Then one day focus is gone, patience is thin, and small issues feel overwhelming. That is not random. That is accumulated internal debt coming due. The only way to reduce that debt is to start honoring standards early and often.

The BreakForth Mindset upgrades the architecture, not just the symptoms.

A BreakForth Practice Tool: The Inner Architecture Audit

Use this tool weekly. Write the answers, not in your head.

1. Where is mental noise showing up right now?
2. What thought keeps looping?
3. What am I interpreting as threat that might actually be information?
4. What boundary have I been avoiding because I do not want to disappoint someone?
5. Where am I over-functioning instead of building ownership?
6. What standard has slipped, and what has it cost my focus, team, or health?
7. What has been rewarded with my attention that should be handled at a different level?
8. What would regulated leadership look like this week in real behaviors?

This tool is not about becoming softer. It is about becoming clearer, steadier, and more effective.

Three Inner Architecture Upgrades That Change Leadership Fast

Upgrade One: From Accessibility to Alignment Accessibility can be valuable, but constant accessibility creates dependence and disrupts strategic thinking. Alignment builds maturity. Alignment means priorities are clear, standards are consistent, and people know how decisions are made. *Alignment reduces noise without reducing care.*

Upgrade Two: From Reactivity to Regulation Reactivity is often a nervous-system issue, not a moral issue. Regulation creates choice. Regulation supports calm authority. It protects decision quality and protects teams from emotional whiplash. *Regulation does not remove urgency. It prevents urgency from becoming identity.*

Upgrade Three: From Motivation to Structure Motivation fluctuates. Structure holds. Structure protects leaders when emotions shift. It preserves standards. It keeps health from becoming negotiable. It makes leadership consistent. *Structure is the quiet engine of long-term performance.*

The Standards That Protect the Leader

Inner architecture becomes real when it turns into standards. Standards are not intentions. Standards are what you enforce when pressure is present. They are guardrails that protect clarity, health, decision quality, and longevity. Without standards, leadership becomes improvisation. Improvisation is expensive. Here are seven standards that protect the leader. These are practical, implementable, and designed to reduce noise quickly.

1. The Standard of Decision Windows Not every decision deserves immediate attention. Assign time windows to decisions based on consequence. Some decisions are reversible. Some are not. Create a simple rule: reversible decisions move faster, irreversible decisions move with a defined process. This protects you from decision fatigue and protects the business from impulsive swings. It also trains the team to stop escalating everything as if it is a crisis.

A practical start is straightforward: identify three decisions you keep revisiting, set a decision deadline, assign an owner, and schedule one final decision meeting. Clarity reduces chatter.

2. The Standard of Controlled Accessibility Availability is not leadership. It is a resource. Accessibility should be intentional, not automatic. If anyone can reach you at any time, the organization will. Then thinking becomes fragmented and the nervous system stays activated.
Create protected blocks on your calendar for thinking, planning, and recovery. Establish office hours for certain types of escalations. Require that issues come with options, not just problems. This standard does not make you less supportive. It makes you more effective, and it teaches the organization to mature.

3. The Standard of Truth Early Late truth is expensive. When leaders avoid truth, problems grow. When difficult conversations get delayed, misalignment becomes culture. A standard of truth early means issues are surfaced while they are still solvable. It means feedback is given with clarity, not frustration. It means silence is not rewarded and responsibility is. A practical start is simple: ask one consistent question in weekly check-ins, "What is the risk we are not saying out loud yet." Make it safe to answer, then act on what you hear.

4. The Standard of Non-Negotiable Recovery Recovery is not a luxury. It is leadership maintenance. Without it, perception becomes distorted and patience shortens. Many leaders treat recovery like a reward that must be earned. That mindset is a trap. Recovery is what allows you to keep earning.
Set a baseline recovery standard that does not move based on workload. Keep it simple. A cutoff time for email most nights. A weekly protected block for physical activity. A monthly day that is truly off. A vacation that stays a vacation. This standard protects decision quality.

5. The Standard of Health as an Operating Requirement Health cannot be a side project. Treat it like an operating requirement. The leader is a primary asset. When health slips, leadership becomes less stable, even when intentions are good. Poor sleep, poor diet, and constant stress create leadership friction that shows up in tone, judgment, and stamina. Choose one health commitment that is realistic and consistent. Do not aim for perfect. Aim for sustainable. A daily walk. A consistent breakfast routine. Hydration. Vitamins. Small decisions compound. Leaders do not collapse from one bad day. Collapse comes from repeated neglect.

6. The Standard of Emotional Regulation Before Communication
Communication is not just content. It is transfer. Leaders transmit state. If you communicate while flooded, the message may be correct, but the impact will be costly. People will hear pressure instead of clarity. Defensiveness rises and ownership drops.

Set a standard: no major message while emotionally escalated. Pause, regulate, then communicate. This protects relationships, reduces churn, and prevents problems that later require cleanup.

7. The Standard of Clear Ownership Over-functioning is often a sign of unclear ownership. When ownership is unclear, leaders carry what should be distributed. That drains capacity and slows the organization. Clear ownership is not harsh. It is responsible.

Set the standard that every major initiative has a clear owner, defined authority, and a clear success metric. Shared ownership is often diluted. Clarify who decides, who executes, who consults, and who approves. This reduces noise and protects time.

These standards are not about controlling people. They are about controlling what leadership allows. They protect the leader from becoming the bottleneck, the emotional shock absorber, or the constant rescue system. They also build a culture that can execute without depending on constant presence.

Internal architecture strengthens every time a standard is enforced, consistently. That is what makes the leader sustainable.

Why This Matters for the Next Chapter

Inner architecture is not about self-improvement for its own sake. It is about leadership that can carry weight without losing clarity. It is about building a leader who can lead through complexity without becoming scattered.

Clarity, execution, and culture all depend on this. Identity depends on this. When inner architecture is weak, identity becomes fragile. When identity is fragile, leadership becomes inconsistent. That is why the BreakForth Mindset builds the inner world before it demands more outcomes.

This chapter is the bridge between potential and sustainability. It is the difference between a breakthrough season and a breakthrough life. Internal structure helps you carry weight. Identity determines how you carry it, and whether you stay anchored when outcomes shift, expectations rise, and pressure intensifies.

The next chapter focuses on identity, because when a leader's identity is unclear, structure eventually gets negotiated, and leadership becomes inconsistent again.

BREAKFORTH PRINCIPLE #4:
Structure Protects Breakthrough

Breakthrough is not sustained by inspiration. It is sustained by internal architecture. Build your inner world with disciplined thinking, regulated responses, spiritual grounding, and clear standards, so your leadership can carry more without losing itself.

CHAPTER 5

What You Tolerate Will Define You

Leadership is revealed less by what you demand and more by what you permit. Many executives can articulate standards in a meeting, speak confidently about culture, and set ambitious targets. Then tolerance quietly rewrites everything. Tolerance becomes the real policy. It becomes the real culture. It becomes the real ceiling.

Tolerance is not always weakness. Fatigue can drive it. Conflict avoidance can drive it. A desire to be fair can drive it. Kindness can drive it. But tolerance still produces outcomes. It shapes the organization. It shapes the team. It shapes the leader.

The BreakForth Mindset treats tolerance as a diagnostic. Whatever you tolerate consistently is what you are agreeing with. That agreement might not be written in a strategy document, but it will show up in execution, morale, and retention. It will also show up in identity, because identity is not only what you believe about yourself. Identity is what you consistently allow around you. What you tolerate will define you.

Tolerance Is an Identity Issue Before It Is a Management Issue

Many leaders try to correct tolerance problems with better systems. Better performance plans. Better communication templates. Better meeting rhythms. Those tools help, but tolerance rarely starts as a process gap. It usually starts as an identity gap.

I remember sitting at my desk when the phone rang, and the caller ID showed the name of an employee I used to dread hearing from. My heart started beating faster, and I could feel stress rise in my body before I even picked up. This person's personality was strong, and their tone could be unnecessarily sharp. Over time, those calls started to feel like conflict, even when I did not have all the facts.

What made it worse is that an impulsive thought came up immediately. I'm just going to answer and say yes to whatever is asked. I don't care. That thought startled me, because it was not leadership. It was avoidance disguised as peacekeeping.

I assumed I knew what the call was about because our new Paid Time Off policy had just gone into effect, and exceptions were not an option. Still, apprehension showed up. Then a sobering realization followed. Why am I hesitant to answer the phone when this is my company, the one I built from the ground up. Why does this feel like being a school kid trying to get to the bus before the bell rings to avoid a fight?

The instinct to delay was strong. Another instinct surfaced alongside it, the urge to answer and over-explain, hoping diplomacy would protect me from discomfort. That is where tolerance often starts. Not with a big decision, but with a small internal negotiation where discomfort gets treated like danger. And when a leader starts managing emotions instead of enforcing standards, the organization pays for it. Inconsistent enforcement creates confusion, resentment, and quiet erosion of trust, especially among high performers who are watching closely.

Right there at my desk, a decision had to be made. Culture had to be protected, and policies had to mean something. Before answering, I committed to setting the tone first. The call would be framed by culture standards, and the conversation would stay within what was acceptable, just like it had on a previous call with that same employee. Not harshly, just clearly. Not emotionally, just firmly.

So I answered.

And the employee said, "Happy New Year, Ms. Early. I just wanted to say I appreciate working for such a great company that cares about us. I got your holiday card, and I wanted to say thank you."

Relief came, but the bigger win was internal. The shift was not about the employee. The shift was about me. Emotional power had been handed away before the conversation even started, and that moment exposed it. Leadership cannot be governed by dread. Standards cannot be enforced only when comfort is present. Culture cannot be protected if tolerance sits in the driver's seat.

I would rather answer the phone with clarity than allow our corporate culture to be compromised. That is what identity does. It keeps standards consistent even when emotions fluctuate.

Identity is not your title. It is not your role. It is not the version of you the market applauds. Identity is the internal agreement you hold about who you are, what you are worth, and what you are responsible for. It determines whether you can make an unpopular decision without shrinking. It determines whether you can receive feedback without spiraling. It determines whether you can hold a standard consistently when someone pushes back.

When identity is unclear, tolerance rises. Standards get negotiated to preserve comfort. Direct conversations get avoided to protect image. Decisions get delayed to reduce exposure. Communication turns into over-explaining to prevent misunderstanding. Misalignment stays in place because confrontation feels heavier than the consequences, at least in the moment.

That is how organizations drift. Not because leaders are evil or incompetent, but because leadership is unanchored.

The BreakForth Mindset insists on a harder truth. Culture is built by what leadership allows. Identity is reinforced by what leadership tolerates.

The Hidden Tax of Tolerance

Tolerance is not neutral. It charges interest.

It charges interest in time, because issues that should have been addressed in one conversation turn into a month of meetings. It charges interest in morale, because high performers notice when standards are uneven. It charges interest in speed, because teams become cautious when consequences are inconsistent. It charges interest in trust, because people stop believing what leadership says when leadership does not enforce it.

Tolerance also charges interest in the leader. Every tolerated misalignment becomes emotional weight. It sits in your mind during meetings. It shows up as irritation, impatience, and fatigue. It makes leadership feel heavier than it needs to. A common sentence shows up in leadership conversations. I don't know why I feel so drained. Sometimes the answer is not complicated. Too much is being tolerated.

Where Tolerance Shows Up First

Tolerance often shows up in predictable places. Not always dramatic, but always revealing.

- Tolerating underperformance because addressing it feels uncomfortable.
- Tolerating disrespect because the person is "valuable".
- Tolerating miscommunication because being direct feels demanding.
- Tolerating chaos because urgency has become normal.
- Tolerating emotional immaturity because conflict feels exhausting.
- Tolerating low accountability because being liked feels safer than being clear.

Each one of these choices signals something. It signals what leadership believes is acceptable. It signals what leadership believes can be corrected. It signals what leadership believes is worth confronting.

Tolerance is never just about the other person. It is also about the leader's internal agreement. Tolerance around high performers is often the most dangerous of all. Leaders hesitate to confront a star employee because results are strong. Deadlines are met. Clients are happy. At the same time, that person may be eroding culture through disrespect, inconsistency, or emotional volatility.

When talent gets a different standard, quiet resentment grows in the rest of the team. High performers who are also healthy start to ask, "Why should I keep giving my best when bad behavior is being rewarded."

That is how organizations lose their most grounded people, not because of pay, but because of uneven standards.

The Approval Trap and Why It Produces Tolerance

Approval is expensive. Not because approval is always wrong, but because needing it becomes a hidden tax. It slows decisions. It weakens communication. It produces over-explaining. It produces hesitancy. It makes standards negotiable.

Most leaders do not admit they want approval. Approval often gets dressed up as collaboration and consensus.

Sometimes it is healthy collaboration. Sometimes it is fear wearing corporate language. Approval seeking shows up in predictable ways:

- Avoiding direct feedback because being liked feels safer than being clear
- Delaying decisions to spread responsibility
- Softening standards to avoid pushback
- Tolerating underperformance to preserve harmony
- Over-preparing because criticism feels like danger

Approval seeking is not a personality flaw. It is often a learned survival strategy. It is what happens when identity is still tethered to being accepted rather than being aligned.

The BreakForth Mindset does not teach leaders to become cold or unapproachable. It teaches leaders to become anchored. Warmth stays. Excellence stays. Relationships stay. Validation becomes optional.

When validation is optional, standards become enforceable.

A Corporate Vignette: When Standards Start Working Again

I once watched a leader in a high-visibility role lose credibility, not because skill was missing, but because standards kept shifting. In one meeting, the leader sounded bold. In the next, cautious. With one group, speed was promised. With another, careful process. The intent was to keep everyone comfortable. The result was predictable. No one trusted the direction.

Eventually a moment came when a decision had to be made. The market was shifting and the organization needed a clear call. The leader paused, then said something simple. "Here is what we are doing. Here is why. Here is what will not change even if we get pushback. Here is what I need from each of you."

The room got quiet, then something changed. Volume did not increase. Anchoring did. The decision was not perfect, but it was clear. Execution improved because uncertainty reduced. Standards started working again because negotiation stopped. That is what identity does. Identity produces steadiness. Steadiness produces trust. Trust increases speed.

Tolerance Reveals the Leader's Inner Agreements

Identity is built through agreements. Agreements are internal commitments that show up in self-talk, boundaries, and follow-through. They show up in what you tolerate, what you confront, and what you postpone. They show up in what you do when nobody is watching.

Some leaders operate with identity agreements they never chose. They were inherited. I have to prove myself. I cannot make mistakes. I have to be strong. I cannot disappoint people. I must be needed. Those agreements may have helped in earlier seasons, but in executive leadership, those agreements create pressure, not power. A BreakForth Mindset leader chooses identity agreements intentionally.

Here are a few examples:

- I lead from alignment, not anxiety.
- I do not negotiate standards to protect comfort.
- Warmth and firmness can exist at the same time.
- Correction does not diminish my value.
- Dislike does not cancel responsibility.

These agreements are not slogans. They are operating commitments. When repeated, they become behavior. When behavior becomes consistent, identity becomes stable. A stable identity reduces tolerance of what should not live in the organization.

Faith, Identity, and the Courage to Correct Early

For faith-rooted leaders, tolerance can become complicated. Kindness matters. Grace matters. Patience matters. But tolerance is not always grace. Sometimes it is avoidance wearing spiritual language.

Faith strengthens identity because it anchors the leader beyond outcomes and opinions. It keeps worth from being outsourced to numbers. It keeps pushback from being interpreted as rejection. It keeps the leader steady enough to correct early rather than waiting until frustration forces a harsh moment.

Correction given early is often gentler than correction delayed. Delayed correction tends to become emotional. Early correction is usually clearer and more constructive.

This is part of what it means to lead with spiritual maturity in corporate environments. Standards can be held without shame. Accountability can be direct without disrespect. Emotional punishment is not required, and cultural compromise is not an option.

A BreakForth Practice Tool: The Tolerance Audit

This tool is designed to be simple and uncomfortable in the right way. Use it weekly or anytime internal friction shows up.

1. What am I tolerating right now that I would advise another CEO not to tolerate?
2. What standard have I communicated but not enforced?
3. What conversation am I avoiding, and what is it costing the business?
4. What am I afraid will happen if I correct this directly?
5. Is that fear realistic, or is it identity-based?
6. What is the next right action that protects the standard without disrespect?
7. What does my future self wish had been confronted earlier?

This audit does not exist to make leaders harsh. It exists to make leaders honest.

The Line Between Patience and Permission

Patience is strategic. It gives people room to grow. It supports learning. It recognizes that development takes time.

Permission is different. Permission is when repeated misalignment stays in place. Permission is when standards become optional. Permission is when high performers start questioning whether excellence matters here.

The BreakForth Mindset draws a clear line. Patience supports growth. Permission produces drift.

Strong culture requires patience with development and firmness with standards. Both can exist in the same leader. Both can exist in the same conversation.

Every leader should have one sentence that anchors them when tolerance tries to creep in. Mine is simple: "I will not allow results to excuse behavior that damages our culture." Saying it does not make the conversation easy, but it removes confusion. It reminds me that I am responsible not only for outcomes, but for the environment that produces those outcomes.

What You Enforce Shapes Who You Become

Tolerance is not only shaping the organization. It is shaping the leader. Every avoided truth weakens identity. Every enforced standard strengthens identity. Every time clarity is chosen over comfort, conviction becomes more stable.

Leadership growth is not only about skills. It is about standards. It is about enforcing what matters before it becomes a crisis.

This chapter is also a bridge. The next chapters will go deeper into faith, growth, and grit, and how belief becomes currency in corporate environments. None of that holds if standards keep slipping. None of that works if tolerance keeps rewriting culture.

The BreakForth Mindset is not built for leaders who want to be admired. It is built for leaders who want to be aligned, effective, and consistent.

BREAKFORTH PRINCIPLE #5:
Standards Reveal Identity

What you tolerate becomes a message, a culture, and a ceiling. Enforce what aligns with your values early, clearly, and consistently, so your leadership and your organization are defined by standards, not drift.

CHAPTER 6

God, Growth, and Grit: A CEO's Inner Trifecta

Leadership at the highest levels is not sustained by talent alone. Skill matters. Strategy matters. Execution matters. But leaders who last, and leaders who grow without losing themselves, carry an internal framework that holds under pressure. That framework is not always visible, but it is always active.

For faith-rooted executives, there is a specific combination that strengthens leadership in a way most corporate development programs do not address. God, growth, and grit. Not as slogans. Not as personality traits. As an operating trifecta.

God is the anchor. Growth is the discipline. Grit is the stamina.

Remove God, and leadership becomes overly dependent on outcomes, reputation, and control. Remove growth, and grit turns into striving and repetition. Remove grit, and growth stays theoretical, because change always costs something.

This chapter is about building an inner framework that can carry corporate life without losing spiritual or moral integrity, emotional stability, or executive effectiveness. It is also about building a leader who can handle pressure without transferring it, handle success without becoming addicted to it, and handle criticism without becoming defensive.

What This Trifecta Protects You From

Before breaking down each component, it helps to name what this trifecta is designed to prevent. Without an internal framework, pressure does not simply stress a leader. Pressure shapes a leader. It shapes tone. It shapes judgment. It shapes priorities. It shapes relationships. It shapes culture. God, growth, and grit protect a leader from three common leadership collapses.

The first collapse is control masquerading as responsibility. This is when leadership becomes tight, anxious, and overly involved. Delegation shrinks. Oversight increases. The leader becomes the bottleneck and calls it excellence.

The second collapse is image management masquerading as influence. This is when a leader starts prioritizing perception over truth. Standards get softened. Feedback gets delayed. Decision-making becomes political. The leader becomes more careful than clear.

The third collapse is fatigue masquerading as strength. This is when exhaustion gets treated as evidence of commitment. Recovery gets postponed. Health slips. Patience shortens. Emotional reactivity increases. The leader keeps moving, but clarity declines.

This trifecta prevents those collapses by anchoring identity, upgrading patterns, and strengthening endurance.

God: The Anchor That Stabilizes the Leader

A faith-rooted leader does not have the luxury of living in two separate lives, one spiritual and one professional. The boardroom does not erase calling. Pressure does not erase purpose. Market shifts do not erase assignment.

God as an anchor means identity is not negotiated with every outcome. Worth is not measured only by revenue and recognition. Decisions are made with discernment, not panic. Leadership becomes accountable to something higher than ego and urgency.

Many leaders say they trust God, but pressure reveals what is actually being trusted. When everything feels dependent on one person, the body carries leadership like a burden. Anxiety rises. Control increases. Delegation shrinks. Rest starts to feel irresponsible. That posture is common, but it is not sustainable. God as anchor does not eliminate responsibility. It eliminates false responsibility. It clarifies what is yours to carry and what is not.

There is also a deeper layer to that anchor for me. Leadership is not status. Leadership is stewardship. That means decisions are not only about what is profitable, but what is principled. Not only what is fast, but what is wise. Stewardship keeps leadership clean. It reminds me that people are not tools for outcomes. They are human beings. And when pressure rises, panic cannot be my language and control cannot be my comfort.

God as anchor also creates a different kind of calm. Not passive calm. Governed calm.

Governed Calm: Composure With Command

Governed calm is not "being chill." It is composure with command. It is the ability to stay internally regulated while still being decisive, direct, and accountable. It is what happens when your nervous system is not driving the meeting, your ego is not driving the message, and your values are driving the decision.

Most leaders know the feeling of the opposite. Your chest tightens after an email. You reread a message three times and still feel provoked. You walk into a meeting already bracing for conflict. Your mind starts racing through worst-case scenarios. Your tone gets sharper than you intended, or you over-explain to protect yourself. That is not a character flaw. It is often a nervous system response, and it is trainable.

Under pressure, the brain can shift toward a more reactive state, which makes it easier to respond emotionally and harder to think with calm precision. Governed calm is the ability to stay in an executive brain state long enough to choose your response. Emotional intelligence reinforces this with a simple principle: feelings are data, not directives. The feeling may be real, but it does not get to run the meeting.

For faith-rooted leaders, governed calm is also stewardship. Stewardship says, "I will not transfer my anxiety to the room." It says, "I will not punish people emotionally because I am under pressure." It says, "I will lead from integrity, not self-protection."

In those moments, I remind myself that the room does not need my adrenaline. It needs my accuracy. It does not need my emotions driving the outcome. It needs my discernment driving the decision. That is a spiritual discipline for me. It is also a leadership discipline. The goal is not to appear calm. The goal is to be governed, so my words carry clarity and my presence does not transfer stress.

Governed calm shows up in behaviors people can feel. You pause before responding, even when urgency is loud. You ask one clarifying question before making one clarifying statement. You communicate facts and expectations without emotional leakage. You correct early, without aggression, and without delay.

Composite Executive Vignette: Governed Calm in the Room

I have watched this play out in executive rooms more than once. A high-stakes situation hits. A critical client is escalating. Revenue is at risk. The team is tense, and everyone is waiting to see whether leadership will panic or lead.

One executive in the room does something simple that changes the entire temperature. There is no rush. No performance urgency. Facts get taken in, and one clarifying question separates signal from noise. Then the situation gets summarized in plain language. No dramatics. No blame. No emotional leakage.

Ownership gets assigned with calm authority. Not as a demand, but as a decision. What will be true by the end of the day is named. What decisions must be made is named. What communication must go out is named. A standard for tone and accountability is set, and the room follows it because the leader's nervous system is not broadcasting threat.

After the meeting, people do not leave more anxious. People leave clearer. What matters is clear. Ownership is clear. The leader is steady. That steadiness becomes contagious, and it protects performance. That is governed calm. It is not passive. It is regulated leadership under pressure, and it is one of the most valuable skills a CEO can develop.

Here is a practical, in-the-moment tool that protects governed calm when pressure spikes:

Name it: "I feel triggered, rushed, or defensive."
Ground it: two slow breaths, then identify the one fact that is true right now.
Choose it: "What does the standard require?" not "What does my emotion want?"

That is governed calm. Not silence, not softness. Leadership that stays regulated enough to stay accurate.

Governed calm is a leadership advantage. It steadies communication. It reduces emotional whiplash. It strengthens culture.

People trust leaders who do not perform stress.

Growth: The Discipline That Keeps Leadership Current

Growth is not a motivational phrase. Growth is a discipline. It is the willingness to update your leadership as your business, your team, and your influence expand.

Many leaders reach a level of success, then stop growing internally. The business keeps changing, but leadership keeps repeating old patterns. What worked at ten employees starts breaking at fifty. What worked at fifty becomes dangerous at one hundred. Strengths become weaknesses when the environment changes.

Growth requires humility, not insecurity. It requires the ability to say, I have done well, and I have more to learn. It requires the ability to receive feedback without defense. It requires the ability to upgrade systems, upgrade standards, and upgrade self.

Growth also requires honesty. Certain patterns cannot be coached away until they are owned. Avoidance. Control. People-pleasing. Over-functioning. These patterns often look like dedication. Sometimes they are simply fear in a productive outfit.

The BreakForth Mindset treats growth as a leadership maintenance requirement. Skill development. Emotional maturity. Communication refinement. Health discipline. Spiritual grounding. None of these are optional if the goal is sustainable influence.

Growth also has a practical business effect. Leaders who keep growing reduce organizational drag. They make faster, cleaner decisions. They correct earlier. They build stronger leaders instead of building dependency. They stop repeating the same issues in new packaging.

A quick truth about growth: growth is not what you intend. Growth is what you practice. Without practice, leadership development becomes content consumption. Reading and listening can be helpful, but only practice builds capacity.

Grit: The Stamina to Hold the Line

Grit is often misunderstood. Many people confuse grit with grinding. Grinding is constant force. Grit is sustained resilience with intelligence.

Grit is the stamina to hold standards when pressure rises. It is the ability to keep doing the right things even when results are delayed. It is the capacity to recover from setbacks without losing identity. It is the commitment to keep learning, keep adjusting, and keep leading.

Grit matters because leadership is full of resistance. Resistance shows up as delays, criticism, betrayal, market shifts, missed targets, and internal politics. Without grit, leadership becomes fragile. With grit, steadiness increases, adaptation improves, and progress continues.

Grit also has a spiritual layer for faith-rooted leaders. It is the decision to stay aligned even when the environment is loud. It is the choice to keep integrity when shortcuts are available. It is the refusal to let fatigue rewrite values.

Grit does not mean ignoring limits. It means honoring purpose with discipline. There is a difference between grit and grinding. Grinding ignores limits and calls it commitment. Grit respects limits and calls it stewardship. Grinding keeps pushing even when the body, mind, and relationships are breaking. Grit knows when to rest so that the next push is intelligent, not desperate.

Leaders who confuse grinding with grit burn themselves out and train their teams to see exhaustion as loyalty. Leaders who understand grit model sustainable pace and show their teams that rest is not weakness.

It is strategy. It means the leader does not quit emotionally, even when outcomes are slow. It also means the leader does not use pressure as an excuse to abandon standards.

A Corporate Vignette: When the Pressure Got Personal

A senior leader once shared that the hardest part of leadership was not the work. The hardest part was what leadership did to their inner life. Strategy was manageable. Meetings were manageable. Responsibility was manageable. But criticism started feeling personal. Delays started feeling like disrespect. Conflict started feeling threatening, and retaliation began to feel justified.

The job followed them home mentally, then emotionally. Sleep suffered. Patience shortened. Relationships strained. The team started feeling the tension, because emotional pressure has a way of leaking into culture.

That leader did not need another leadership book. An internal framework was missing. Pressure needed to be carried without being transferred.

That is where God, growth, and grit become real. God anchors identity. Growth updates patterns. Grit holds the line.

Without that trifecta, pressure becomes personal, and personal pressure turns into personal problems and performance problems.

The Trifecta in Practice: What It Looks Like in Real Leadership

God, growth, and grit show up in specific behaviors. Not vague concepts, but observable leadership patterns.

God shows up as discernment. Decisions are made with clarity, not panic. Boundaries are honored. Integrity is protected. Worth is not outsourced to outcomes.

Growth shows up as coachability. Feedback is received with maturity. Patterns are examined. Skills are upgraded. Leadership becomes more effective, not more defensive.

Grit shows up as consistency. Standards are enforced. Hard conversations happen early. Recovery is honored. The leader stays steady through resistance.

When these three work together, leadership becomes both powerful and sustainable. It also becomes easier for teams to trust what leadership says, because leadership stops changing tone with every pressure wave.

The Trifecta Operating Rhythm: Daily, Weekly, Quarterly

This is where many leadership frameworks fall short. They sound good, but they do not become a rhythm. The BreakForth Mindset is designed to become a rhythm. Here is a simple operating rhythm that makes the trifecta practical.

Daily Anchor Start with a short reset that reinforces stewardship. Ask: What am I carrying today that is not mine to carry. Then ask: What standard must I hold today no matter what the day brings. This daily anchor protects identity before emails and meetings start shaping it for you.

Weekly Growth Action Choose one growth action per week that is visible. One coaching conversation. One hard conversation you have been delaying. One skill refinement. One boundary reset. The goal is not intensity. The goal is consistency.

Quarterly Grit Review Once per quarter, identify what pressures have been trying to talk you out of your standards. Then decide what gets reinforced and what gets removed. Many leaders keep old patterns because they never review them. Grit is not only endurance. Grit is the refusal to repeat what no longer works.

This rhythm is simple on purpose. The power is repetition. A simple weekly pattern can anchor this.

On Monday, reset with God and your priorities before the week's demands set them for you.

On Wednesday, recalibrate by asking what needs to be adjusted based on what has already unfolded.

On Friday, review where you honored your standards and where you did not.

Small, consistent check-ins like this keep God, growth, and grit from becoming ideas. They become an actual way of life.

A BreakForth Practice Tool: The Trifecta Audit

Use this tool weekly. Write the answers. Do not rush.

1. Where have I been operating as if everything depends on me?
2. What outcome has been affecting my identity more than it should?
3. What leadership pattern needs to be updated, not excused?
4. Where is discomfort trying to talk me out of standards?
5. What does integrity require right now, even if it is inconvenient?
6. What is one growth action I will take this week, with specificity?
7. What is one grit action I will take this week, with consistency?

This audit keeps the trifecta practical. It prevents faith from becoming vague, growth from becoming theoretical, and grit from becoming force.

The Business Consequence of Neglecting the Trifecta

When God is not the anchor, leadership defaults to control, anxiety, and image management. When growth is not practiced, rigidity increases and outdated patterns repeat. When grit is missing, inconsistency rises and standards start slipping.

The business consequence shows up quickly. Confusion rises. Culture weakens. Turnover increases. Execution slows. Trust erodes. Fatigue starts shaping decisions. The BreakForth Mindset does not separate spiritual maturity from leadership maturity. It treats them as connected.

A leader who is anchored, growing, and resilient becomes a stabilizing force in the organization.

Why This Matters for the Next Chapter

The next chapter is about the belief economy, and why faith becomes corporate currency. Not in a religious sense, but in the way steadiness, conviction, and discernment create trust. Organizations pay for leaders who can carry pressure without panic, hold standards without drama, and communicate with maturity when others are reactive.

The leader who can do that becomes a market advantage.

BREAKFORTH PRINCIPLE #6:
Anchor First, Then Advance

God anchors the leader, growth keeps leadership current, and grit sustains execution under pressure. This trifecta protects identity, strengthens standards, and produces leadership that can scale without losing itself.

CHAPTER 7

The Belief Economy: Why Faith Is the Corporate Currency

Every organization operates on an economy. Not only a financial economy, but an internal economy. An economy of trust. An economy of credibility. An economy of confidence. An economy of belief.

Executives already know what happens when confidence drops. Teams hesitate. Decision cycles slow down. Risk tolerance collapses. People start protecting themselves instead of building outcomes. Even strong strategies lose power when belief is weak.

This is why faith, properly understood, becomes corporate currency. Not as religious language in the workplace. Not as performance spirituality. Faith as the disciplined ability to hold steady under pressure, interpret reality without panic, keep integrity when shortcuts are available, and lead without transferring anxiety to everyone around you.

In the BreakForth Mindset, faith is not decoration. It is a leadership advantage because it strengthens the belief economy every organization depends on.

The Belief Economy Is Always Operating

Belief shows up in how leaders speak and decide. It shows up in whether initiative is encouraged or suppressed. It shows up in whether accountability is clear or avoided. It shows up in whether teams move with confidence or stall in hesitation. When belief is strong, teams move. When belief is weak, teams stall.

Belief is corporate currency because it changes what an organization can do under pressure. Strong belief creates momentum, courage, speed, and honesty. It makes resilience practical when the quarter is hard and the market noise is louder than the mission.

To understand what an organization truly believes, skip the survey at first. Start with the places where people hesitate and the truths people delay. Is it safe to surface issues early. Do standards hold when pressure hits. Does leadership project calm authority or emotional volatility. Are decisions made with clarity, or postponed until urgency forces a scramble.

Belief is not what the company says on the wall. Belief is what the company expects will happen when someone takes a risk.

Defining the Belief Economy

The belief economy is how much trust and confidence people have in leadership, and it decides how fast they buy in, how openly they tell the truth, and how reliably they deliver.

It is not soft. It is structural. The belief economy influences performance because it shapes perception, and perception shapes behavior. Three components determine whether belief rises or drops in an organization.

Consistency Consistency is standards plus follow-through. It is leadership that does what it says. It is priorities that do not change every week without explanation. It is accountability that feels predictable, not selective.

Safety Safety is not comfort. Safety is psychological permission. It is the ability to surface issues early without punishment. It is the confidence that mistakes become feedback, not shame. It is the freedom to speak honestly without fear of public embarrassment.

Signal Signal is leadership communication that reduces noise. It clarifies what matters, what success looks like, and what is urgent versus important. It is the leader's ability to communicate direction without emotional leakage.

When these three are strong, belief rises. When they weaken, belief drops. The organization still functions, but it functions with hesitation, politics, and hidden drag.

Faith as Stability, Not Hype

Faith is often misunderstood because people associate it with hype. Faith is not hype. Faith is not ignoring facts. Faith is disciplined trust that allows a leader to face reality without falling apart, spinning, or performing.

Faith gives a leader a different internal posture. It makes room for clear thinking when outcomes are uncertain. It keeps fear from hijacking tone. It keeps urgency from turning into panic. It keeps the leader from needing to control everything just to feel safe.

A faith-rooted leader can look directly at a missed target and still speak with clarity, because identity is not hanging on one metric. A faith-rooted leader can face a tough market and still make decisions without desperation, because pressure is not interpreted as a personal threat. A faith-rooted leader can experience resistance and still keep integrity intact, because shortcuts do not become tempting just because the quarter gets tight.

That is why faith matters in corporate leadership. It produces steadiness that teams can lean on. It produces restraint that protects the organization from reactive decisions. It produces courage without bravado, the kind that tells the truth early, makes the hard call, and holds the standard when it would be easier to compromise.

Faith also changes how a leader communicates. It creates language that is firm without being sharp. It creates accountability without humiliation. It creates confidence that does not require pretending. It creates the ability to say, "Here are the facts. Here is the plan. Here is what will not change," without transferring anxiety to the room.

Faith is not a substitute for competence. It is a stabilizer for competence. It keeps competence from getting contaminated by fear, ego, or image management. It allows competence to stay clean when pressure rises, and when the environment is loud, it helps the leader remain accurate.

The Real Asset: Trust Under Pressure

Trust is not built only in good seasons. Trust is built in pressure seasons. Trust is built when leaders do not disappear. Trust is built when leaders do not perform. Trust is built when leaders tell the truth early, hold standards consistently, and communicate without emotional leakage.

This is why faith is corporate currency. Faith allows leaders to remain steady when outcomes are uncertain. It allows leaders to tell the truth without fear. It allows leaders to correct without anger. It allows leaders to hold the line without panic.

Trust under pressure becomes an asset. It reduces turnover. It increases execution speed. It protects culture. It strengthens client confidence. It stabilizes decision-making.

Organizations do not only pay for strategy. Organizations pay for stability.

I once watched a client choose to renew with a company that had a slightly higher price, even though a competitor underbid aggressively. When asked why, the client said, "I know they will tell me the truth when something goes wrong. I do not have to guess what is real." That answer had nothing to do with features. It had everything to do with belief. The client believed in the company's steadiness. The belief economy was strong, so the relationship could handle tension.

A Corporate Vignette: When the Room Followed the Steadiest Person

I have been in rooms where everyone was intelligent and accomplished, but the environment was still unstable. A crisis was unfolding. Data was coming in incomplete. The team was tense. People were talking fast. Everyone wanted to be first to respond.

Then one leader slowed the room down. Not by dominating it, but by stabilizing it. Facts were requested. Signal got separated from noise. What was known and unknown was named. A decision point was set. Ownership was assigned. The tone carried stewardship, not panic.

The room followed that leader because steadiness created safety. The team could think again. The team could execute again. The leader did not bring hype. The leader brought clarity. That is the belief economy at work. The steadiest leader becomes wealthy in trust.

Belief Debt, The Hidden Cost of Inconsistency

Most leaders understand financial debt. Belief debt is similar, but it accumulates quietly. Belief debt forms when trust is spent faster than it is replenished. It builds when leaders promise and do not follow through. It builds when priorities change without explanation. It builds when standards get enforced selectively. It builds when misalignment is tolerated publicly but addressed privately. It builds when urgency gets rewarded more than integrity.

Belief debt also accumulates through confusion. Too many messages. Too many shifting priorities. Too many "quick changes" without clear ownership. Teams start anticipating reversals and protecting themselves.

The danger of belief debt is that it does not show up immediately. Results can still be strong for a season. People still show up. Meetings still happen. Projects still move. But commitment starts thinning. Truth gets filtered. Initiative becomes cautious. The organization becomes less honest and less bold, even while appearing productive.

Then someone tries to correct it with a speech. That usually fails, not because the speech is wrong, but because belief debt is not paid with words. It is paid with consistency.

Paying down belief debt requires visible follow-through. Clear standards. Predictable accountability. Calm leadership under pressure. Trust does not return because it is demanded. Trust returns when evidence becomes consistent again.

Faith and Risk, How Leaders Make Better Decisions

Risk is part of leadership. Risk is unavoidable in growth. The question is not whether risk exists. The question is how leaders respond to it.

Leaders with weak belief economies tend to respond to risk in two unhealthy extremes. Either avoiding risk completely, or taking reckless risk to feel powerful. Both are costly.

Faith produces a third option. Disciplined courage.

Disciplined courage is not bravado. It is not impulsive risk. It is the ability to move forward with integrity when the outcome is not guaranteed, while still respecting facts, trade-offs, and consequences. Disciplined courage refuses panic and refuses paralysis at the same time.

It shows up when a leader names what is known and unknown, chooses a responsible next action, and communicates with calm authority. It shows up when standards are enforced even when the room is uncomfortable. It shows up when gambling is rejected, and stalling is rejected as well.

Disciplined courage strengthens the belief economy because it trains people to trust leadership decisions. Teams become more willing to speak early because truth is handled responsibly. Decision cycles shrink because clarity replaces fear.

Faith-based leadership does not gamble. It governs.

The Faith Advantage in Culture

Culture is shaped by what leaders reward, tolerate, and enforce. Faith, when mature, strengthens those choices because it keeps leaders anchored in values under pressure.

A faith-rooted leader is more likely to protect integrity when shortcuts are available. More likely to correct early rather than delay until frustration rises. More likely to maintain standards without emotional punishment.

Faith does not make leaders perfect. It gives leaders an internal reference point beyond convenience. That reference point strengthens culture.

Culture follows belief, and belief follows leadership behavior.

Belief Signals, A Fast Diagnostic for Leaders

Leaders often ask, "How do I know whether belief is strong right now." Look for signals before looking for numbers. Numbers usually confirm what belief has already done. Here are belief signals you can observe within a week:

- Are problems surfaced early, or hidden until they become expensive.
- Are decisions clean, or political.
- Are meetings getting shorter with clearer outcomes, or multiplying without closure.
- Are people proposing solutions, or only reporting issues.
- Are leaders delegating with confidence, or rechecking everything.
- Are standards consistent, or shifting based on personalities.
- Is accountability direct, or softened and delayed.

Belief is not only what people say. It is how people behave when the stakes are real. When belief rises, initiative rises. When belief drops, self-protection rises.

A BreakForth Practice Tool: The Belief Economy Audit

Use this tool when uncertainty rises, when morale feels shaky, or when leadership pressure increases.

1. What belief is the team holding right now about the future?
2. What belief is my communication reinforcing, stability or fear?
3. Where have standards become inconsistent, and what message did that send?
4. What truth needs to be said early, before it becomes expensive?
5. What am I modeling, urgency or stewardship?
6. What decision is being delayed because approval feels safer than clarity?
7. What would strengthen trust in the next seven days?

This tool helps leaders manage the belief economy intentionally, not accidentally.

The Business Consequence of a Weak Belief Economy

When belief is weak, execution slows. People disengage quietly. Teams avoid accountability. Feedback becomes filtered. Risk tolerance collapses. Innovation stalls. The organization starts operating in self-protection rather than mission.

A weak belief economy also shows up outside the company. Clients sense instability. Partners sense inconsistency. Stakeholders sense hesitation. Trust erodes, even when the product is strong.

The belief economy is not a motivational concept. It is an operational reality. It determines how quickly an organization can move without breaking trust.

Belief is felt before it is measured. Teams can feel when leadership is stable, even before engagement scores are tallied. Clients can feel when a partner is steady, even before contract renewal conversations occur. People sense whether they can rely on what a leader says. The metrics eventually confirm it, but the feeling shows up first. Wise leaders pay attention to the emotional climate long before the dashboard catches up.

Belief Compounds, How to Build It in 7 Days

Belief does not usually rise because of one big speech. Belief rises because of consistent signals. Small actions, repeated with clarity, change what people expect. When expectations change, behavior changes. When behavior changes, results follow. Here is a practical seven-day reset that strengthens the belief economy quickly. It is not a marketing plan. It is leadership behavior with intention.

Day 1: Clarify one priority and one standard. Name the single most important outcome for the week, and name one standard that will not be negotiated. Keep it simple. When priorities are clear and standards are real, noise drops.

Day 2: Tell one hard truth early. Surface the issue that everyone senses but nobody has named. Use plain language. Avoid drama. Early truth prevents expensive truth later.

Day 3: Delegate one decision with clear ownership. Choose one decision you usually hold too tightly. Assign an owner, define authority, and set a deadline. Belief rises when people see trust paired with accountability.

Day 4: Remove one source of noise. Cancel a meeting that produces no outcomes. Stop a recurring update that is no longer useful. Consolidate communication into one clear channel. Noise reduction is belief protection.

Day 5: Reinforce one cultural standard publicly. Recognize behavior that reflects the culture you want. Address a misalignment calmly if it needs correction. Consistency is credibility.

Day 6: Close one open loop. Finish the decision that has been lingering. Send the follow-up that keeps getting delayed. Resolve the ambiguity that is causing hesitation. Open loops drain belief.

Day 7: Acknowledge progress and reset priorities. State what moved forward, what was learned, and what needs adjustment. This is not celebration for optics. It is clarity for momentum.

Seven days will not fix everything. It will change the signal. And once the signal changes, belief starts compounding.

BREAKFORTH PRINCIPLE #7:
Trust is Currency

In every organization, belief drives behavior and behavior drives results. Faith strengthens the belief economy by producing steadiness, integrity, and disciplined courage under pressure. Leaders who build trust become wealthy in influence.

CHAPTER 8

Destiny by Design: Building the Life and Business You See

Many leaders live by default. Not because of laziness, but because pressure is loud and time is short. Calendars fill. Meetings stack. Problems demand immediate attention. Before long, leadership becomes responsive instead of intentional. Hard work stays high, but direction gets blurry, and that blur has a cost. Time gets wasted, focus gets diluted, and the organization learns how to move without real alignment.

Beneath the noise is destiny, the outcome your life and leadership are capable of producing when talent is matched with alignment and calling is matched with discipline. It is not a mystical idea. It is the future you are responsible to build, and the standard that exposes when your pace is busy but not purposeful. Productivity can still be off course. Admiration can still sit on top of misalignment.

Destiny by design is the refusal to drift. It is leadership with intention. It is the discipline of seeing clearly, deciding deliberately, and executing consistently, even when priorities compete and interruptions are constant. That discipline requires personal investment. Not only in strategy, but in the leader. Clarity strong enough to say no. Identity strong enough to hold standards. Energy managed well enough to sustain effort. Skill sharpened enough to execute. Integrity steady enough to stay aligned when shortcuts are available. Without those investments, vision stays inspirational, and the leader stays tired.

This chapter is not about fantasy. It is about design. Design is what happens when vision becomes structure. It is how a leader turns what they can see into what they can deliver. It is the choices that protect focus, the systems that reduce drag, and the standards that keep execution clean. It is also the rhythm that keeps progress moving after motivation fades, because motivation is not a strategy.

The BreakForth Mindset does not treat vision as a motivational exercise. It treats vision as leadership responsibility. If direction is not designed, pressure will design it for you, and pressure rarely designs anything you will be proud to sustain.

Vision Is a Leadership Requirement

Vision is often framed as inspiration. In real organizations, vision is operational. Vision tells people what matters. Vision sets priorities. Vision gives context for decisions. Vision reduces politics because direction becomes clear.

When vision is missing, everyone creates their own version of what matters. That is how misalignment spreads. That is how resources get wasted. That is how fatigue increases even when people are working hard.

A leader does not need a perfect vision statement. A leader needs a clear direction that can be communicated, reinforced, and protected. Direction must be stable enough to guide decision-making and specific enough to shape execution.

Three questions keep vision operational. Where are we going. Why does it matter. What will it require from us. When those answers are clear, execution gets cleaner and teams move with fewer interruptions.

Design Means Structure, Not Just Ideas

Many leaders have ideas. Many leaders have goals. The difference is design.

Design turns vision into a system. It decides what priorities stay, what distractions get removed, and what standards protect execution. Design is not a one-time plan. It is a repeatable process that keeps leadership from improvising under pressure.

Destiny by design requires three layers. A clear picture of the outcome. A disciplined plan that can be executed. A leadership rhythm that keeps the plan alive. Without rhythm, vision becomes a yearly document that teams stop believing.

I have also seen what happens when leaders avoid design. I was speaking with one of my CEO friends and he shared how he declared a bold three-year vision. When we spoke a few months later, he said he felt like nothing was changing. I said did you change structure, priorities, or decision rights to align with the vision. He said, "No." That was the challenge. Old meetings stayed. Old reporting lines stayed. Old habits stayed. And that's why within a year, the vision felt like a slogan no one believed. It was not that his vision was wrong. There was no design underneath it. People learned that nothing meaningful would change, so their effort adjusted to match. Dreams without design eventually turn into disappointment.

I can remember when BreakForth Solutions hit our ten-year anniversary. Everyone was ecstatic. Our HR generalist at the time wanted to plan a big celebration, and I understood why. Ten years is not small. Ten years means perseverance, credibility, and proof that the business is real.

But the truth is, I did not feel like celebrating.

That milestone felt less like a finish line and more like a checkpoint. Ten years forced a question I could not avoid. What got us here, will it carry us where we are going. In that moment, the issue was not whether success had been achieved. The issue was whether the way I was leading could support the next decade.

A quiet truth became obvious. Accessibility had turned into dependency. Decision-making was running through me. Too much rework was landing on my desk. The organization was growing, but I could feel myself becoming a bottleneck. That was not because the team lacked talent. The structure still treated me like the point of contact for too many things.

So instead of planning a party, I started redesigning.

Time got redesigned. Accessibility got redesigned. Frameworks got implemented to reduce rework and force clearer ownership. Then a decision got made that changed the shape of the business. It was time to hire a Vice President of Operations. It was time to restructure areas that should no longer be reporting to me and move them under that leader. The goal was not to step away from leadership. The goal was to step into the right kind of leadership.

Within about three months, the difference was real. Pressure lightened. Decisions got faster. Focus returned. Cash, culture, and customers became clear again. Energy shifted because the company was no longer running through one person's nervous system. Leadership became more scalable because ownership became more real.

Destiny by design looked like that. Not inspirational language. Structural leadership decisions. The decision to stop being stuck in execution forever and build a company that could carry the next level without breaking the leader.

In hindsight, a celebration in that moment would have been fitting. Still, the bigger celebration is what followed. More stability. More speed. Better leadership coverage. A clearer path. Renewed confidence that the next decade is not just possible, it is buildable.

The Inner Picture Shapes the Outer Outcome

A leader's internal picture matters more than most people admit. The internal picture shapes decisions before the leader ever speaks. It shapes what gets funded. It shapes what gets tolerated. It shapes what feels possible.

This is why Chapter 3 mattered. Belief sets the ceiling. If the leader cannot see the outcome as carryable, the organization will feel hesitation. If the leader can see it clearly and communicate it consistently, belief rises and execution improves.

Destiny by design is not pretending. It is disciplined imagination paired with disciplined execution. The goal is not to "manifest." The goal is to build. Building requires clarity, trade-offs, and a willingness to stop negotiating the future down to what feels safe.

A Corporate Vignette: When Vision Finally Became Real

I once watched a company stay stuck for years because the leadership team kept changing priorities. Every quarter brought a new focus. Every meeting introduced a new initiative. Employees stopped asking what mattered because the answer kept changing.

Then a new leader stepped in and did something simple. Three priorities were chosen for the year. The priorities were communicated clearly. A fourth priority could not be added unless something was removed. A standard for decision-making got enforced. If a project did not align with the priorities, it did not get funded. If a meeting did not serve execution, it got canceled.

Within months, the organization felt different. People moved faster because guessing stopped. Teams collaborated more because competition for attention decreased. Morale improved because effort started producing visible progress. Vision became real because the environment was designed to support it.

The Design Framework: See, Decide, Build

Destiny by design stays grounded when vision becomes a process. Here is a framework that keeps it practical.

See: Seeing is clarity. It is the ability to define the outcome in plain language. What does success look like. What changes when the vision is achieved. What is different in the business, the culture, the leader, and the life. Seeing is not daydreaming. Seeing is defining. It is naming what matters most and refusing vague language that allows drift.

Decide: Decision is where many leaders stall. Decisions require trade-offs. Decisions require saying no. Decisions require protecting standards. Identity is involved here. Leaders who need approval struggle to decide because decisions invite critique. Leaders who are anchored can decide with calm authority, name trade-offs honestly, and move forward without needing everyone to agree.

Build: Building is execution. It is consistent action supported by systems, ownership, and accountability. It is not bursts of effort. It is rhythm. Destiny becomes real in the build phase. That is where most people lose momentum. Consistency is harder than visioning. Structure matters because it keeps progress moving when excitement fades and when pressure tries to pull attention back into urgency.

Design Requires Trade-Offs

Every designed life and business is built on trade-offs. Trade-offs are not punishment. Trade-offs are focus.

You cannot build everything at once. Saying yes to every opportunity dilutes standards. Protecting health, culture, and growth requires hard choices about time and access. Trade-offs are what separate leaders who grow intentionally from leaders who stay busy.

The question is not whether trade-offs will be made. The question is who will make them. A leader who refuses to decide will still experience trade-offs. The difference is that pressure will choose them instead.

A designed leader decides what gets attention, what gets delegated, what gets postponed, and what gets eliminated.

Clarity is not only what you pursue. Clarity is what you refuse.

Design Standards That Protect Destiny

Design becomes real when it turns into standards. Standards keep vision from being negotiated down by pressure, personalities, or constant urgency. Without standards, even a clear direction gets diluted. Execution becomes reactive again, and the leader ends up back in drift. These design standards are simple on purpose. They are meant to be implemented, not admired.

The Priority Standard: No more than three priorities at a time. If a fourth priority appears, something gets removed. This forces focus and protects teams from whiplash.

The Meeting Standard: Meetings must produce a decision, alignment, or removal of a blocker. If none of those outcomes exist, the meeting gets redesigned or canceled. Time is too expensive for motion without meaning.

The Ownership Standard: Every major initiative has one clear owner with authority, a deadline, and a success measure. Shared ownership often becomes diluted ownership. Clear ownership reduces rework and escalation.

The Accessibility Standard: Access to the leader is structured, not constant. Office hours, escalation rules, and solution-oriented communication protect strategic thinking. Constant availability creates dependence and interrupts design work.

The Review Standard: A weekly review protects momentum. A monthly review protects alignment. A quarterly review protects strategy. Without review rhythms, drift returns quietly.

These standards do not make leadership rigid. They make leadership clean. They create the conditions where destiny can be built on purpose, not by accident.

A BreakForth Practice Tool: The Destiny by Design Audit

Use this tool monthly. Write the answers.

1. What am I building right now, intentionally or by default?
2. What outcome am I claiming, and what action supports it?
3. What is draining focus that should be removed or delegated?
4. What standard must be enforced for the next level to be possible?
5. What is one decision I have delayed that is costing momentum?
6. What does my calendar reveal about my real priorities?
7. What belief ceiling is still trying to negotiate my vision down?

This tool keeps the leader honest. It reconnects vision to execution, and it exposes where drift is still being tolerated.

Business Implication: Designed Leaders Reduce Organizational Drag

Organizational drag shows up as rework, hesitation, unclear ownership, and constant escalation. Designed leadership reduces drag. It creates fewer priorities, clearer ownership, and faster decisions. It also creates culture stability because standards are consistent. A leader who designs does not create a perfect plan. A leader who designs creates a clear path. That path reduces confusion, reduces churn, and increases the likelihood that effort produces progress.

A simple question can change the way a leadership team meets around vision. At least once a quarter, ask, "What have we changed in our structure, priorities, or standards that proves we are serious about where we say we are going." If the room gets quiet, design has not caught up to what is being declared.

BREAKFORTH PRINCIPLE #8:
Vision Requires Design

Vision becomes destiny when it is structured, protected, and executed with discipline.
See clearly, decide deliberately, and build consistently.

CHAPTER 9

From Stuck to Unstoppable: Breaking the Bottleneck

Every growing organization reaches a moment where progress slows, not because the market is closed, but because the internal system cannot carry the next level. Timing gets blamed. The environment gets blamed. Capacity gets blamed. Often, the simplest word is the right one: bottleneck.

A bottleneck is not a bad season. It is a constraint. It is the narrowest point in the system that determines the speed of the whole organization. Money can be available. Demand can be present. Strategy can be sound. Execution still slows when one constraint remains unresolved.

Talent gaps have been the biggest bottleneck I've seen at BreakForth as we scaled. The work expanded. Expectations increased. Delivery demanded specialized capability. The bench did not always keep pace. Strong culture and strong mission still cannot compensate for missing capacity forever.

Here is what that drag feels like in real leadership. The calendar tightens, then it starts to suffocate. The same two or three people get pulled into everything because they are the safest hands. Rework increases because the wrong level is doing the wrong work. Delegation starts to feel risky, not because people are unwilling, but because coverage is thin. Decisions slow down because the people who should be owning them are overloaded. Pressure comes from two sides at once, delivery demands performance while the gaps demand attention.

That combination creates a dangerous pattern. Strategy gets postponed to cover execution. Culture work gets delayed because urgency keeps winning. The leader stays busy, but the business starts feeling stuck. Vision is not the issue. Constraint is.

The BreakForth Mindset does not treat bottlenecks as excuses. It treats them as signals. Bottlenecks reveal what the next level requires.

Talent Gap Signals: How to Know the Bottleneck is Here

Talent gaps are not always obvious at first. The signs show up in patterns.

A recurring quality issue appears in the same place, even when effort is high. Escalations increase because ownership is unclear or overloaded. Meetings multiply because decisions are not being made cleanly at the right level. High performers start carrying two roles, then three. Leadership keeps jumping into delivery work, not as an exception, but as the default. Onboarding gets rushed because seats need filling. Retention becomes shaky because pressure stays high and relief stays late.

Those signals are not personal failures. They are capacity warnings.

The Real Definition of a Talent Bottleneck

A talent gap becomes a bottleneck when the work outgrows the team's current capability faster than the organization can build or acquire that capability.

That is not an insult to the team. It is a reality of scaling. A company can have excellent people and still be under-resourced for the next level. Growth changes the talent equation. Roles become more specialized. Standards rise. Volume increases. The margin for error shrinks.

A talent bottleneck does three things. Execution slows. Rework increases. Leadership gets pulled into coverage personally. That last dynamic is where risk grows, because executive attention starts getting consumed by work that should be handled through systems, layers, and ownership.

A CEO should not be the bridge for missing capacity. The CEO should be the builder of the system that prevents missing capacity from turning into chaos.

How Talent Gaps Create Invisible Drag

Talent gaps often show up before anyone says the words out loud. Meeting volume increases because clarity is missing. Escalations rise because ownership is weak. Deadlines slip because people are overextended. Leaders start checking more because trust feels risky. Strong team members burn out because they are carrying two loads. Then the organization starts adjusting downward. Targets get softened. Standards get negotiated. Innovation slows. Leadership becomes more conservative. Vision did not disappear. Capacity got stretched.

This is the part many executives do not name clearly. Talent gaps can shrink vision. Design work gets replaced by survival work. That is not leadership failure. That is leadership under constraint.

The BreakForth Mindset calls for a different response. Identify the gap. Name it plainly. Build a plan that closes it. Protect that plan with standards.

A Corporate Vignette: The Contract Was Won, Then the Pressure Hit

I have watched this happen in more than one organization. A major contract gets won and the celebration is real. The opportunity is legitimate, the numbers look strong, and the mission impact feels meaningful. For a moment, it feels like momentum has finally caught up to vision.

Then delivery reality arrives and the tone shifts. The work requires specialized skills and immediate readiness, while the client expects performance from day one. The internal team is talented, but stretched. A few key positions are still unfilled, and other seats are filled by people who are capable but still ramping into the complexity of the work. The gap is not a lack of effort. Coverage is the issue.

Pressure rises fast because delivery does not wait for hiring to catch up. Leaders start compensating to protect outcomes. Oversight becomes heavier, not because leaders want control, but because risk feels too high to ignore. Weekends get consumed, meetings stack, and urgency becomes the operating tone. In that environment, the organization is still moving, but it is moving in a way that is costly.

The opportunity was not wrong. The bottleneck was ignored. Talent gaps do not stay quiet because they sit at the narrowest point of execution. Attention gets pulled from wherever it is available. Most often, that means pulling it from the CEO and the few strongest leaders, until strategy gets postponed and leadership becomes the stopgap.

That is when growth starts feeling heavy. Growth is not the problem. Insufficient capacity is the problem, and until it is addressed, the organization keeps paying through rework, fatigue, and slowed momentum.

A BreakForth Moment: When the Gap Landed on the CEO

There was a season at BreakForth when the gap showed up in my day before I could explain it cleanly. Decisions kept coming back to me that should have been resolved at a lower level. Review cycles got longer because the right expertise was not consistently available. A few high performers carried more than was sustainable, and the strain showed up in small ways, tone, responsiveness, energy, and patience.

At first, the temptation was to push harder. Work longer. Stay more available. Jump into the weeds so standards stayed intact. That impulse makes sense when a leader cares. A trap forms quickly, because the more the CEO jumps in, the more the organization learns to rely on the CEO as the safety net. Over time, that pattern becomes culture.

A different choice had to be made. The gap could not be covered forever. It had to be closed. Not with pressure, but with structure.

Why Talent Gaps Are So Hard to Fix

Talent gaps are difficult because they touch multiple realities at once. Hiring takes time. Clearance and compliance requirements add complexity in many environments. Budget constraints exist. Culture must be protected. Performance must stay stable while onboarding happens.

Another factor makes this harder. Hiring becomes reactive when it should be strategic. The organization tries to solve a year-long capacity issue in a month. Quality drops. Retention drops. The wrong hires get made, and the bottleneck returns in a different form.

Closing talent gaps requires discipline. Planning ahead of demand. Role clarity. Bench development. Leadership coverage that prevents the CEO from becoming the default solution. A predictable pattern shows up when talent gaps persist. The leader starts lowering the bar in small ways. Standards slip, not because values changed, but because fatigue makes compromise feel practical. That is when culture takes a hit. The short-term seat gets filled and long-term trust gets damaged.

It is important to remember that talent is not headcount. Talent is coverage, capability, and continuity. Coverage answers the question, "Do we have enough people in the right seats." Capability answers, "Do those people have the skills this level requires." Continuity answers, "Can we sustain this without constantly starting over." An organization can be fully staffed on paper and still be under-talented for the work it has committed to deliver.

The Three Talent Levers: Build, Buy, Borrow

Every executive has three levers to close a talent bottleneck. Strong leaders use all three with intention, and the choice depends on timing, risk, and consequence.

Build develops internal talent through training, mentorship, stretch assignments, and leadership development. Build works best when capability can be developed within a reasonable timeframe and the team has enough bandwidth to learn without burning out. Building protects culture and retention, and it strengthens the bench for the future.

Buy means hiring. Buy works best when the skill is mission critical, timelines are tight, and internal development cannot close the gap fast enough. Buying requires selection discipline and clarity. A great hire still fails without defined expectations, authority, and onboarding.

Borrow means contracting, consultants, fractional leadership, or partners. Borrow works best when speed is required, when the skill is temporary, or when bridge coverage is needed while recruiting. Borrowing can protect delivery and buy time, especially when hiring would otherwise be rushed.

Over-relying on one lever creates imbalance. Building alone can be too slow. Buying alone can damage culture if selection discipline slips. Borrowing alone can create dependency and prevent internal capability from forming. A mixed strategy closes gaps while protecting standards.

Fixing Talent Gaps Without Lowering Standards

Under pressure, some leaders lower standards to fill seats. That move is understandable and expensive. A bad hire is not neutral. Morale takes a hit. Client trust weakens. Time gets consumed. Rework becomes normal. High performers get tired of carrying the cost.

A better approach protects standards and strengthens the pipeline. Better sourcing. Better screening. Clear role definition. Strong onboarding. More intentional development for internal talent. Fast correction when misalignment appears.

Culture can be protected while hiring quickly. Discipline is what makes that possible. Role expectations must be clear before posting. The first thirty days must have a scorecard that is measurable.

Feedback must be direct and early. Course correction must happen before frustration becomes tone. Clear leadership does not require harshness. It requires standards.

Speed matters. Standards matter more.

A simple thirty-sixty-ninety approach can make closing talent gaps more manageable.

In the first thirty days, clarify the roles and gaps with precision and decide which capabilities are non-negotiable.

In days thirty to sixty, execute on hiring, development, or contracting decisions that directly target those capabilities.

In days sixty to ninety, stabilize the changes by reinforcing expectations, giving early feedback, and adjusting workloads so that the new structure can hold.

The point is not to fix everything in three months. The point is to prove that the bottleneck is being addressed, not ignored.

A BreakForth Practice Tool: The Talent Bottleneck Diagnostic

Use this tool when execution feels heavier than it should. Write the answers.

1. Where is performance slipping because capability is missing, not because effort is low?
2. Which roles are overloaded because coverage is thin?

3. What work is being done by senior leaders that should be handled at the right level?
4. What is the cost of this gap in rework, delays, and leadership distraction?
5. Which capability must be added in the next 30 to 90 days to protect delivery?
6. What can be built internally, and what must be hired externally?
7. What is the retention risk if this gap stays open another quarter?

This diagnostic forces clarity. It turns frustration into a plan.

The Bottleneck That Hurts Growth the Most

The most dangerous talent bottleneck is leadership coverage. When a company grows, leadership layers must grow. When layers do not grow, the CEO becomes the hub. The hub becomes the constraint. Decisions slow. Teams wait. Execution becomes dependent on access.

This is why hiring a Vice President of Operations, a strong program lead, or a strong functional leader can be a breakthrough move. It shifts the operating model. It restores flow. It also protects the CEO from becoming the default problem solver.

The CEO is not meant to be the escalation path for everything. The CEO is meant to be the designer of the system that handles escalations properly.

The Business Consequence of Closing the Bottleneck

When talent gaps close, execution speed increases. Rework decreases. Decisions become cleaner. Leaders regain time for strategy. Culture stabilizes because accountability becomes more consistent. Teams feel less frantic because coverage becomes real. This is why talent is not an HR problem. Talent is an executive priority. Talent is capacity.

A strong strategy with weak talent coverage becomes a stress machine. A strong strategy with strong coverage becomes a growth engine.

Why This Matters for the Final Chapter

Breaking bottlenecks is one of the most practical ways to increase influence without increasing chaos. When bottlenecks are addressed, momentum returns. Leadership becomes more stable. Vision becomes more buildable. Standards become easier to enforce.

Stewardship shows up here. Closing talent gaps is not only about productivity. It protects people. It protects culture. It protects the leader's capacity to lead at the right level, with clarity and endurance.

The final chapter is a charge to the leader. Not a motivational close, but a call to operate in the BreakForth Mindset with maturity and consistency.

Momentum is not an accident. It is built.

BREAKFORTH PRINCIPLE #9:
Capacity Creates Momentum

Bottlenecks reveal what the next level requires. Close talent gaps with disciplined hiring, development, and leadership coverage, so execution can flow without exhausting the leader or breaking the culture.

CHAPTER 10

You're the Leader We've Been Waiting For

Waiting is one of the most socially acceptable ways to stay small. It rarely looks like fear. It often looks like patience, professionalism, and being "reasonable." Many leaders spend years waiting for the right opportunity, the right title, the right endorsement, or the right moment to feel ready. The waiting becomes a habit, and the habit becomes a story. The story sounds mature, but underneath it is often a quiet agreement: someone else gets to decide when I am allowed to lead.

That agreement does not just slow careers. It slows lives. It keeps leaders in environments that benefit from their loyalty but do not honor their potential. It keeps talented people over-preparing and under-owning. It keeps decision-makers looking outward for validation when the work of leadership requires internal authority.

Waiting is not always wrong. Timing matters. Preparation matters. Wisdom matters. Yet waiting becomes dangerous when it turns into delay. Delay turns into drift. Drift turns into regret. A leader can be busy, respected, and competent, and still be drifting because direction is being negotiated instead of chosen.

The BreakForth Mindset is not a mindset for leaders who want to be noticed. It is a mindset for leaders who are ready to be responsible. It is a leadership posture that says, "I will not wait for permission to become who I am called to be." It chooses alignment over applause, standards over comfort, and discipline over wishful thinking.

This final chapter is not designed to hype you. It is designed to anchor you. The principles in this book are not theories. They are leadership infrastructure.

Consistent application does not only change outcomes. It changes the leader who is producing the outcomes. That is the only kind of transformation that lasts.

The BreakForth Mindset Is a Decision, Not a Personality

Leadership is not a personality trait. Charisma can help, but charisma does not hold when pressure rises. Confidence can help, but confidence can be performative when identity is fragile. Loudness can get attention, but attention is not the same thing as influence.

Leadership is a decision backed by discipline. It is the decision to think clearly when emotion is loud. It is the decision to hold standards when tolerance feels easier. It is the decision to tell the truth early instead of protecting comfort. It is the decision to lead people without transferring anxiety to them. It is the decision to keep integrity intact when shortcuts are available.

The BreakForth Mindset is not a style. It is a standard. It is a set of choices that shape how you think, how you interpret pressure, how you decide, how you set boundaries, how you build teams, and how you sustain integrity. It trains leaders to stop outsourcing stability to circumstances. It trains leaders to remain consistent when the environment is inconsistent. It removes the need to be validated as a condition for being decisive.

Clarity is magnetic. Consistency is magnetic. Teams do not follow leaders because leaders are perfect. Teams follow leaders because leadership feels stable. That stability comes from internal agreement, not external applause.

Proven Principles, Real Transformation, and the Ninety-Day Window

The BreakForth Principle was not formed overnight. It was birthed out of years of experience as a CEO. It was forged through pressure, decisions, consequences, mistakes, wins, and the kind of growth that cannot be learned through theory alone. It came through moments when I had to tell the truth early, hold the standard, and choose the next level even when it was uncomfortable.

That detail matters because leaders often want fast change with no structure. Real transformation is not magic. It is consistent application. The same principle that applies to business applies to leadership maturity. What gets repeated gets reinforced. What gets reinforced becomes behavior. What becomes behavior becomes culture, whether that culture is personal or organizational.

Ninety days is enough time to feel the difference when these principles are applied with discipline. The goal is not perfection. The goal is consistency. Within ninety days, perception can become clearer. Standards can become firmer. Decisions can become cleaner. Leadership can become steadier. Culture can become healthier. Momentum can return, not as a feeling, but as an operational reality. A leader will not become a different person in ninety days. A leader can become a more aligned version of themselves in ninety days.

Alignment is what changes everything because it simplifies leadership. It reduces internal noise. It reduces emotional leakage. It increases the ability to decide and execute without hesitation.

A Leader's Assignment Is Not to Be Chosen, It Is to Choose

Many leaders do not fail because they lack capability. Many leaders stall because someone else's approval still feels like the final gate. That is why so many capable people stay stuck. They keep preparing, keep producing, keep waiting, and keep hoping the right people will notice. In some environments, that notice will never come because the decision was made before the interview started.

I know what that feels like.

Before opening BreakForth, I worked for a large information technology contractor. Nearly eight years had been invested there, and I knew I wanted more than what my current position was offering. The Program Director role was the goal. Preparation was not casual. Training had been completed.

Certifications had been earned. Events had been attended. Volunteer commitments had been accepted. Visibility had been built. The work had been done.

Applications went in for several openings. For the position I wanted most, the Business Area Director committed to interview me with one of the section Vice Presidents. Confidence walked into that room because my contributions were real. Familiarity was assumed. Recognition was expected. The interview felt like it should be straightforward.

Then they asked a question that caught me off guard, not because it was difficult, but because it revealed something. "Have you managed the finances for a large contract over one hundred million dollars."

My portfolio at the time was about fifty million, so I answered honestly. I had not managed a one-hundred-million-dollar contract, but the principles of financial management would be the same because programs operated on the same financial framework. Their response did not sound curious. It sounded dismissive. The conversation shifted into a list of reasons I was not "ready." Then they said that a PMP certification would be helpful and at least seven years of experience in the business organization was required.

Shock hit because the information was wrong. I already had the PMP certification. The company had paid for it. I had held it for three years at that point. Experience was not a gap either. More than seven years had been invested in the organization. Several other certifications and accomplishments were already in place. In that moment, the truth became clear. The interview was a formality. They had not read my resume. They had not come prepared to consider me seriously.

A different version of me could have turned around and corrected them sharply. Bias could have been confronted. Errors could have been exposed. Anger could have been justified. That was not the move. I stood up quietly to leave and said one sentence that held dignity and truth at the same time. "When you get an opportunity, please read my resume."

A few weeks later, staying there no longer made sense. Another meeting happened so we could mutually agree on my transition and departure. What followed was the birth of BreakForth Solutions, now a multi-million dollar IT and professional services firm that I own one hundred percent of. That happened for one reason. Instead of waiting for them to choose me, I chose to lead.

What That Moment Teaches Every Leader

That moment was not only a career turning point. It was an identity turning point. Preparation is necessary, but permission is optional. Some environments benefit from your patience but do not respect your potential. Staying in a place that refuses to see you eventually shrinks you, no matter how qualified you are. The shrinking does not always look dramatic. It often looks like compromise. Lower expectations. Reduced confidence. Smaller decisions. A quieter voice. Less imagination. More caution than conviction.

Another lesson came through that moment. Leaving was not the only act of courage. Courage also showed up in refusing to let their misjudgment become my definition. Their failure to read my resume did not change what I had built. Their refusal to choose me did not reduce my capacity. Their bias did not get to become my boundary.

That is the BreakForth Mindset in real life. It is the refusal to let someone else's blindness become your ceiling. It is the willingness to move forward without needing endorsement from the same environment that benefits from keeping you in place.

The BreakForth Commitments: The Ninety-Day Standard

A final chapter should not only inspire. It should equip. Insight without application becomes entertainment. Transformation requires structure. Structure requires commitment.

The next ninety days can become a turning point if leadership is treated like an operating system instead of an emotional moment. These commitments are not slogans. They are actions that can be practiced until they become normal. Each one builds on the chapters that came before it, and each one strengthens a leader's ability to carry influence without losing stability.

A first commitment is to lead from conviction rather than mood. Conviction keeps leadership stable when emotions fluctuate. It creates standards that can be enforced and truth that can be spoken early. It holds decisions in alignment with values rather than pressure. A leader who leads from conviction does not change tone based on who is present or what is trending. Consistency becomes a form of trust.

A second commitment is to treat pressure as information rather than identity. Pressure will come. The difference is interpretation. Facts must stay separate from fear. Ownership must stay separate from over-functioning. Clarity must stay separate from adrenaline. Pressure does not have to define leadership. It can refine leadership when perception is disciplined.

A third commitment is to break the lid and build belief on purpose. Belief does not change through wishing. Belief changes through repetition, evidence, and disciplined agreements. If a ceiling has been operating in your leadership, name it and replace it with a standard. The replacement must be practiced until it becomes reflex. This is how capacity expands and confidence becomes stable.

A fourth commitment is to build internal architecture before demanding bigger outcomes. Inner structure determines sustainability. Without structure, success becomes heavier. With structure, growth becomes cleaner. Health, boundaries, recovery, and regulation are not luxuries. They are leadership requirements. Structure protects the leader from becoming reactive and protects the organization from becoming dependent on one person's nervous system.

A fifth commitment is to stop tolerating what is shrinking you. Tolerance is not neutral. It writes culture and it writes identity. What should be corrected must be addressed early. What must be enforced must be enforced consistently. Avoiding discomfort does not prevent conflict. Avoidance often delays it until the cost becomes higher.

A sixth commitment is to operate with disciplined courage. Disciplined courage tells the truth early, makes the hard call, and holds standards even when discomfort is present. It is faith with structure. It is courage that respects facts and discipline that refuses paralysis. This is how risk becomes governed rather than avoided or dramatized.

A seventh commitment is to design destiny rather than drift into it. Design requires trade-offs. Focus requires saying no. Execution requires rhythm. Destiny becomes real when vision becomes structure, and structure becomes consistent action. A leader who designs does not wait for perfect conditions. A leader who designs builds conditions that support progress.

An eighth commitment is to close the bottleneck instead of covering it. Capacity creates momentum. Talent gaps and leadership coverage gaps do not disappear through effort. They disappear through structure, hiring, development, and ownership. Covering a gap can work temporarily. Living in gap coverage eventually drains the leader and trains the organization to rely on rescue instead of systems.

Each commitment is simple to understand. Application is where maturity shows up. The difference between leaders who grow and leaders who plateau is not intelligence. Willingness is often the separator. Willingness to lead when it is uncomfortable. Willingness to stop negotiating standards. Willingness to choose alignment even when approval is not guaranteed.

The next ninety days will shift your leadership if you apply these commitments. To reduce overwhelm, start with a focused thirty-day plan.

In the first ten days, choose one commitment and make it visible. For example, decide that for ten days you will not agree to any decision that violates a standard you have already set.

In the next ten days, add one internal architecture practice, such as a fixed daily reflection block or a weekly review ritual. In the final ten days, address one tolerance issue you have been avoiding. One conversation. One standard enforced. One drift corrected.

At the end of thirty days, look honestly at what feels different. Do you feel more settled or more scattered. Are decisions clearer or still tangled. Has your calendar shifted even slightly toward alignment. Those observations will tell you that the work is not theoretical. It is working in real time.

Your Leadership Is Needed Now

The world does not need more leaders who are impressive. The world needs leaders who are consistent. The world needs leaders who can hold standards without ego and hold truth without panic. The world needs leaders who can build organizations where people can breathe, think, and execute without fear. That kind of environment does not happen by accident. It is designed and protected by leadership.

You are not reading this book because you are average. Something in you knows you were built for more. That is not pride. That is responsibility. Responsibility to lead with integrity. Responsibility to stop hiding behind preparation when action is required. Responsibility to stop waiting for permission when the assignment is clear.

A final question matters here. What would change if leadership stopped being something you hoped to grow into and became something you chose to embody now. Not after the next title. Not after the next season. Not after the next person approves you.

Ownership is the dividing line. The same leader who waits for approval keeps shrinking their future to match other people's comfort. The leader who chooses to lead becomes the one others are waiting for.

You are the leader we've been waiting for, and leadership starts with a decision that is followed by discipline.

BREAKFORTH PRINCIPLE #10:
Choose to Lead

Leadership is not granted by permission. Leadership is sustained by alignment, structure, and disciplined action. Choose conviction over mood, truth over comfort, and design over drift, then lead with consistency until your life and your organization reflect what you were built to carry.

APPENDIX

The BreakForth C.I.R.C.L.E.

The Six Pillars of Inner-Aligned Leadership

The BreakForth C.I.R.C.L.E. is a simple way to remember the core pillars that run through this book. These six dimensions work together to form a complete picture of inner-aligned leadership. They are not steps you complete once. They are a circle you live in and move through again and again as you grow.

When the C.I.R.C.L.E. is intact, leaders are clear, stable, and effective. When one area is neglected, the entire system feels the strain.

C – CONVICTION

Conviction is your internal authority. It is the set of non-negotiable beliefs and standards that govern how you lead when the outcome is uncertain, the room is quiet, and the pressure is high. Conviction keeps you from trading integrity for convenience and long-term purpose for short-term comfort. A leader with conviction does not lead from mood. They lead from principle. Their yes and no have weight, and their team knows what they can count on.

Key Question: What do I believe so deeply that it must not change when pressure shows up?

I — Identity

Identity answers the question: Who am I as a leader, apart from titles, seasons, and other people's opinions? It shapes how you interpret feedback, how you handle resistance, and how you respond when someone misjudges you. When identity is unclear, leadership becomes dependent on approval. When identity is anchored, leadership becomes steady. Decisions stop being auditions. They become expressions of who you are and what you stand for.

Key Question: Am I leading from who I am, or from who I think people need me to be?

R — RESILIENCE

Resilience is the capacity to lead through adversity without losing clarity or character. It is more than pushing through. It is the ability to recover, to reset, and to continue with wisdom after you have been pressed. Resilient leaders do not pretend pressure is easy. They simply refuse to let pressure define them. They know how to interpret setbacks as information, not identity, and they keep moving forward with lessons learned.

Key Question: How do I respond when outcomes do not match my expectations?

C — CLARITY

Clarity turns leadership from noise into direction. It defines what matters, where you are going, and what is required. Clarity reduces politics because it limits space for guessing and second-guessing. It allows your team to focus their energy on execution instead of interpretation. Clear leaders can say in plain language what success looks like and what does not belong. They are able to name trade-offs and priorities without vague statements that leave people confused.

Key Question: Could my team explain our direction and priorities without me in the room?

L — LEGACY

Legacy lifts your focus beyond the next deadline. It is not only about reputation. It is about the impact your leadership has on people, culture, and systems long after you are no longer in the role. Leaders who think about legacy make different choices. They own the fact that their daily decisions are shaping someone else's future workplace and someone else's faith in leadership. They care about how people grow under their watch, not just what they produce.

Key Question: If someone worked under my leadership for five years, who would they be when they left?

E — EXECUTION

Execution is the ability to turn conviction, clarity, and vision into consistent, aligned action. It is where leadership stops being conceptual and becomes visible. Execution is not just getting things done. It is getting the right things done, at the right time, in the right way. Effective execution depends on systems, ownership, accountability, and rhythm. When execution is strong, strategy becomes reality instead of a slide deck.

Key Question: Do our actions, calendars, and decisions actually match what we say is important?

Living in the C.I.R.C.L.E.

The C.I.R.C.L.E. is not meant to be a diagram on a wall. It is meant to be walked. On any given day, you may sense that conviction is strong but resilience is thin. In one season, clarity may be high while execution is scattered. The BreakForth leader pays attention to these shifts and returns to the C.I.R.C.L.E. to ask: Which pillar needs attention now, so that the rest can hold? When you strengthen one pillar, the others benefit. When you neglect one pillar, the others strain. The invitation of The BreakForth Principle is simple and serious. Do not just grow your skills. Build your C.I.R.C.L.E.

The BreakForth Principles: A Quick Reference

All Ten Principles from The BreakForth C.I.R.C.L.E.

Each chapter of this book concludes with a BreakForth Principle, a personal leadership code designed to be lived, not simply learned. They are collected here as a consolidated reference and a daily leadership compass.

BREAKFORTH PRINCIPLE #1: Conviction Is Not Optional

You cannot lead beyond the strength of your internal alignment. Conviction is not optional. It is the non-negotiable infrastructure for sustainable leadership.

BREAKFORTH PRINCIPLE #2: Perception Governs Performance

Pressure does not decide your leadership outcome. Your perception does. Train your lens, regulate your internal state, and lead from clarity, not threat.

BREAKFORTH PRINCIPLE #3: Belief Sets the Ceiling

Your leadership expands to the level of belief you are willing to discipline. Break the lid by training your lens, strengthening self-efficacy, and choosing grounded courage over protective hesitation.

BREAKFORTH PRINCIPLE #4: Structure Protects Breakthrough

Breakthrough is not sustained by inspiration. It is sustained by internal architecture. Build your inner world with disciplined thinking, regulated responses, spiritual grounding, and clear standards, so your leadership can carry more without losing itself.

BREAKFORTH PRINCIPLE #5: Standards Reveal Identity

What you tolerate becomes a message, a culture, and a ceiling. Enforce what aligns with your values early, clearly, and consistently, so your leadership and your organization are defined by standards, not drift.

BREAKFORTH PRINCIPLE #6: Anchor First, Then Advance

God anchors the leader, growth keeps leadership current, and grit sustains execution under pressure. This trifecta protects identity, strengthens standards, and produces leadership that can scale without losing itself.

BREAKFORTH PRINCIPLE #7: Trust is Currency

In every organization, belief drives behavior and behavior drives results. Faith strengthens the belief economy by producing steadiness, integrity, and disciplined courage under pressure. Leaders who build trust become wealthy in influence.

BREAKFORTH PRINCIPLE #8: Vision Requires Design

Vision becomes destiny when it is structured, protected, and executed with discipline. See clearly, decide deliberately, and build consistently.

BREAKFORTH PRINCIPLE #9: Capacity Creates Momentum

Bottlenecks reveal what the next level requires. Close talent gaps with disciplined hiring, development, and leadership coverage, so execution can flow without exhausting the leader or breaking the culture.

BREAKFORTH PRINCIPLE #10: Choose to Lead

Leadership is not granted by permission. Leadership is sustained by alignment, structure, and disciplined action. Choose conviction over mood, truth over comfort, and design over drift, then lead with consistency until your life and your organization reflect what you were built to carry.

The BreakForth Self-Assessment: Where Is Your C.I.R.C.L.E. Right Now?

A Personal Leadership Diagnostic

This self-assessment is designed to help you identify where your inner leadership infrastructure is strong and where it needs intentional development. There are no right or wrong answers. The value is in your honesty. For each dimension, respond to the reflection questions and assign yourself a score from 1 to 5 using the scale below. When you are finished, total your scores and consult the interpretation guide at the end.

1 = Rarely or never true of my leadership right now
2 = Occasionally true, but not consistent
3 = Sometimes true; I am actively working on this
4 = Mostly true; this is a strength with room to grow
5 = Consistently and fully true of my leadership

C – CONVICTION   SCORE: ______ (OUT OF 15)

Conviction is the internal authority that governs your leadership when pressure is high and certainty is low.

1. I lead from a clear set of non-negotiable principles, not from the mood of the room.
2. I make decisions that I can defend on the basis of values, not just outcomes.
3. My team would describe me as consistent, even under pressure.

I — IDENTITY   SCORE: ______ (OUT OF 15)

Identity is the anchor that keeps your leadership steady when circumstances shift and opinions vary.

1. I know who I am as a leader independent of my title, current role, or external validation.
2. I can receive critical feedback without it destabilizing my sense of self.
3. I lead from a place of security rather than a need for approval.

R — RESILIENCE   SCORE: ______ (OUT OF 15)

Resilience is your capacity to recover, reset, and continue with wisdom after adversity.

1. I interpret setbacks as information rather than as evidence of my limitations.
2. I recover from difficult seasons without losing clarity or character.
3. I have practices in place that help me replenish my energy and perspective.

C — CLARITY   SCORE: ______ (OUT OF 15)

Clarity is the discipline of defining what matters, where you are going, and what is required.

1. I can articulate the direction and priorities of my leadership in plain, specific language.
2. The people I lead could explain our goals & standards without me in the room.
3. I regularly communicate what belongs & what does not belong in our focus.

L – LEGACY   SCORE: ______ (OUT OF 15)

Legacy is the long-view discipline of leading with an awareness of the impact you leave on people, culture, and systems.

1. I make decisions with an awareness of how they will shape the people around me long-term.
2. I invest in the growth of the people I lead, not only in their performance.
3. I could articulate what I want to be true of the people and culture I leave behind.

E – EXECUTION   SCORE: ______ (OUT OF 15)

Execution is the ability to translate conviction, clarity, and vision into consistent, aligned action.

1. My calendar, decisions, and priorities consistently reflect what I say matters most.
2. I follow through on commitments with the same discipline I expect from others.
3. I have systems and rhythms that keep my leadership moving forward rather than reacting.

 **YOUR TOTAL SCORE: _______ (OUT OF 90)** 

(75–90) Strong Foundation: Your inner leadership infrastructure is well-developed. Continue deepening your weakest dimension and use this book to sharpen your edge.

(55–74) Active Development: You are building well. Identify the one or two dimensions with the lowest scores and give them focused attention over the next ninety days.

(35–54) Significant Opportunity: Your inner infrastructure has meaningful gaps that are likely showing up in your leadership outcomes. This book is precisely for where you are right now.

(Below 35) Urgent Priority: Your foundation needs significant investment. Do not skip chapters. Work through this book slowly and honestly. The work ahead is worth everything it will require.

Reading Group and Leadership Team Guide

Facilitated Discussion Questions for Each Chapter

This guide is designed for executive teams, leadership cohorts, book clubs, and organizational development programs working through The BreakForth Principle together. Each set of questions is intended to move the conversation from intellectual engagement to personal application.

Introduction: The BreakForth Mindset

1. What drew you to this book? Be specific about what you hoped to find or confront.
2. How would you describe the relationship between your outer performance and your inner leadership infrastructure right now?
3. Which of the six C.I.R.C.L.E. pillars felt most immediately relevant to you when you read the Introduction, and why?

Chapter 1: The Conviction Code: Leading from the Inside Out

1. Describe a recent decision where conviction, not mood or circumstance, determined your response. What made that possible?
2. Where in your current leadership are you most tempted to lead from pressure rather than principle?
3. What is one non-negotiable conviction you would want your team to be able to name about you without hesitation?

Chapter 2: Pressure Isn't the Problem, Perception Is

1. What narrative do you most frequently default to when you are under significant pressure?

2. Describe a situation where reframing the pressure changed your outcome. What shifted?
3. What would change in your team's culture if leaders consistently modeled a growth-oriented response to difficulty?

Chapter 3: Break the Lid: The Neuroscience of Belief

1. What belief about yourself or your organization has functioned as a ceiling in the last twelve months?
2. Where do you see the neuroscience of belief playing out in real time on your team?
3. What would you attempt if you genuinely believed it was possible?

Chapter 4: Built to BreakForth: Architecting Your Inner World

1. How would you describe the current state of your inner architecture, your values, rhythms, self-awareness, and boundaries?
2. What is one structural element of your inner world that needs intentional investment right now?
3. What would your leadership look like if your inner world were as well-designed as your best operational system?

Chapter 5: What You Tolerate Will Define You

1. What have you been tolerating in your leadership or your organization that you know is shaping the culture in ways you do not intend?
2. What standard do you hold for others that you are not consistently holding for yourself?
3. What would change in your team's performance if you raised the standard in one specific area starting this week?

Chapter 6: God, Growth, and Grit: A CEO's Inner Trifecta

1. How do you currently integrate your spiritual grounding with your professional leadership? Are they connected or compartmentalized?
2. In what area of your leadership has grit been most tested in the last year?
3. What does growth look like for you in this season, specifically and practically?

Chapter 7: The Belief Economy: Why Faith Is the Corporate Currency

1. Where in your leadership have you been waiting for evidence before investing belief? What would change if you reversed the order?
2. How does your current level of belief about what is possible affect the people you lead?
3. What is one area where you need to make a faith-forward decision before the full picture is clear?

Chapter 8: Destiny by Design: Building the Life and Business You See

1. Do your daily decisions, calendar, and priorities reflect the life and organization you say you are building? Where is the gap?
2. What is the single most important design decision you need to make in your leadership right now?
3. What would you stop doing if you were truly committed to building what you were designed to build?

Chapter 9: From Stuck to Unstoppable: Breaking the Bottleneck

1. Where do you recognize yourself as the bottleneck in your own leadership or organization?
2. What have you been calling an external obstacle that may actually be an internal limitation?
3. What is the next level of your leadership that you have been avoiding, and what would it cost you to step into it now?

Chapter 10: You're the Leader We've Been Waiting For

1. After reading this book, what is the most honest assessment you can make of the leader you are right now versus the leader you are becoming?
2. What one commitment from this chapter will you make today, not next quarter?
3. What does it mean to you personally to BreakForth?

NOTES

The BreakForth Principle draws on more than two decades of lived leadership experience across corporate, federal contracting, entrepreneurial, and ministry environments. The observations, frameworks, and principles in this book are grounded in that experience, in direct work with leaders across industries, and in a sustained engagement with the broader fields of organizational psychology, leadership development, and applied neuroscience.

Where specific research, data, or ideas from other scholars and practitioners have informed the thinking in these pages, those contributions are acknowledged below. Readers who wish to explore the underlying science of belief, identity, and executive performance further are encouraged to engage works in the areas of neuroplasticity and mindset, organizational behavior, and the psychology of high performance.

Chapter 1: The Conviction Code: Leading from the Inside Out

1. For background on neuroplasticity and the way repeated thought and behavior patterns shape the brain over time, see Christopher S. Green and Daphne Bavelier, "Exercising Your Brain: A Review of Human Brain Plasticity and Training-Induced Learning," Psychology and Aging 23, no. 4 (2008): 692–701.
2. McEwen, B. S. "Central role of the brain in stress and adaptation." Physiology & Behavior/NIH. (2010)
3. For research on stress, emotional regulation, and the brain systems involved in executive functioning, see Amy F. T. Arnsten, "Stress Signalling Pathways That Impair Prefrontal Cortex Structure and Function," Nature Reviews Neuroscience 10, no. 6 (2009): 410–422.

4. Arnsten, A. "Neural Circuits Responsible for Conscious Self-Control." Yale/NIH-hosted article (2012).

Chapter 2: Pressure Isn't the Problem, Perception Is

5. For research on stress and its effect on executive functioning, including the role of the prefrontal cortex and related stress-response systems, see Amy F. T. Arnsten, "Stress Signalling Pathways That Impair Prefrontal Cortex Structure and Function," Nature Reviews Neuroscience 10, no. 6 (2009): 410–422.
6. For the foundational concept of cognitive appraisal in stress and coping, see Richard S. Lazarus and Susan Folkman, Stress, Appraisal, and Coping (New York: Springer, 1984).
7. Girotti, M. et al. "Prefrontal cortex executive processes affected by stress in health and disease." Progress in Neuro-Psychopharmacology & Biological Psychiatry (2017).

Chapter 3: Break the Lid: The Neuroscience of Belief

8. For the concept of self-efficacy and its role in confidence, persistence, and performance, see Albert Bandura, Self-Efficacy: The Exercise of Control (New York: W. H. Freeman, 1997).
9. For a concise overview of Bandura's theory of self-efficacy and human agency, see American Psychological Association, "Self-Efficacy and Human Agency." (1997)

Chapter 6: God, Growth, and Grit

10. For additional research on stress, self-regulation, and cognitive control under pressure, see Amy F. T. Arnsten, "Stress Signalling Pathways That Impair Prefrontal Cortex Structure and Function," Nature Reviews Neuroscience 10, no. 6 (2009): 410–422.

ABOUT THE AUTHOR

Nichelle L. Early is the Founder and President of BreakForth Solutions, Inc., a multi-million-dollar IT and professional services firm that has earned three placements on the *Inc. 5000* list of America's fastest-growing private companies and two placements on the *Inc. Regionals* Mid-Atlantic Fastest Growing Companies lists. She knows what it means to build a company from a single employee to a high-performing team, to carry a complex contract portfolio, and to lead in environments where results and integrity are both non-negotiable.

In addition to her corporate work, Nichelle serves as the CEO of BreakForth Ministries and Consulting, Inc., a 501(c)(3) organization dedicated to ministry, training, and community impact. She also leads several entrepreneurial ventures, all grounded in the same conviction that leaders are at their best when their inner life, spiritual life, and professional life are not at war with one another.

Across boardrooms, conferences, and ministry spaces, Nichelle is known for her ability to speak to both the heart and the operating reality of leaders. Her voice is direct but encouraging, deeply principled but never out of touch with the pressures executives face.

Through The BreakForth Principle, she brings together her experience as a CEO, her calling as a faith-rooted leader, and her passion for human potential to help leaders build the inner strength their organizations need now.

Connect with the Author

Nichelle L. Early is available for keynote speaking, executive leadership development, corporate consulting, and ministry engagements. To inquire about bringing The BreakForth Principle to your organization, conference, or leadership team, please reach out through the channels below.

Speaking and Consulting Inquiries:

info@AlignedAuthorityGroup.com
AlignedAuthorityGroup.com

Online:

Website: AlignedAuthorityGroup.com
LinkedIn: https://www.linkedin.com/in/nichelleearly/
Instagram: @NichelleLEarly
BreakForth Solutions, Inc.
www.BreakForthSolutions.com
BreakForth Ministries and Consulting, Inc.
www.BreakForthMinistriesInc.org

If this book has impacted your leadership, your team, or your organization, Nichelle would love to hear from you. Stories of "breakforth" are the reason this work exists.